◆ T

KILLER

Juliet Gellatley with Tony Wardle

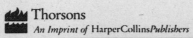

Thorsons
An Imprint of HarperCollins*Publishers*
77–85 Fulham Palace Road
Hammersmith, London W6 8JB
1160 Battery Street
San Francisco, California 94111–1213

Published by Thorsons 1996

10 9 8 7 6 5 4 3 2 1

Front cover design: Greg Walker

A catalogue record for this book
is available from the British Library

ISBN 0 7225 3162 1

Printed in Great Britain by
Caledonian International Book Manufacturing, Glasgow

To my mum with great love and affection.

To Audrey for your faith in me and Viva! and your compassion for the animals.

And to all the animals who suffer silently and those who fight to save them.

Special thanks to Greg for your friendship and artistic wizardry and Graeme for your dedication, talent and unpaid work.

◆ CONTENTS

◆ INTRODUCTION

In 1994 people took to the streets all across Britain. They were determined, passionate and outraged and their actions struck a chord in the hearts of millions. For the first time in memory, animal welfare made headline news every day for months.

The reason for the demonstrations, of course, was the transportation of live animals to Europe – sheep to be fattened for a few days in France or Spain and then killed and labelled 'home produced'; calves, little more than a few days old, to be placed in solitary crates and killed after a few months and sold as veal.

Consistent campaigning had led to P & O Ferries, Stena Sealink and Brittany Ferries, the main cross-channel ferry operators, dropping the export of live animals for slaughter and the street demonstrations were aimed at preventing other, opportunist companies from picking up the abandoned business. These elusive merchants tried every possible outlet by air and sea, using the cover of dawn and dusk to move their fragile cargoes. But everywhere they went, at whatever time of day, people were there to greet them, to stand in their way, to lie in the road, to attack their consciences, to prevent their trade and to thrust the issue into the living-room of every home in the country.

Those who joined together in outrage defied stereotyping. There were middle-aged, middle-class women who had never protested publicly about anything before in their lives, young women in Doc Martens with rings through their noses, senior citizens, and young men in combat jackets with dogs on pieces of string. What they had in common was their anger at the denial of even the most fundamental compassion to living creatures. This unity defied the 16 years of British Government philosophy which proclaimed there is no such thing as society, only individuals, which replaced care and concern with greed and profit, gave legitimacy to exploitation and claimed that only a free market can answer the world's problems – most of which were created by the free market in the first place.

After years of being told that they shouldn't care, these dedicated groups were shouting at the top of their voices that they did care. Not only did their actions challenge Government cynicism, but they also did something much more fundamental: they made previously complacent people confront the intricate relationships between the meat and dairy industries and what is placed on our dining tables.

After an interview I did for BBC TV's *Money Programme* at the start of the demonstrations, the camera operator asked me what was wrong with drinking milk. Like millions of other people, he believed that cows naturally gave milk like chickens lay eggs. He was clearly taken aback when I explained that, just like a woman, cows have to be made pregnant before lactation takes place and their calves are removed so that we can have their milk.

The camera operator wasn't unique. Most of the population were – and largely still are – lacking even the most basic knowledge of where their food comes from, the circumstances of its production and the wider impact it has on the environment and the impoverished of the world. But the live exports coverage has, I believe, started a process of enquiry which is irreversible – it is the beginning of a voyage of discovery.

We have to hope that this voyage will be a rapid one because it is impossible to sustain the anarchy and chaos of a meat-based diet which is literally devouring the Earth. Vegetarianism/veganism is not some old hippy concept rooted in a cannabis-induced nirvana but an idea which has been around for hundreds, even thousands of years. It lies at the heart of virtually every great philosophy and religion and what began as a moral stand now has a frighteningly convincing scientific legitimacy.

Livestock production is at the heart of almost every environmental catastrophe confronting the Earth, from acid rain to global warming, desertification to deforestation. Soil erosion, loss of habitat and water depletion are all intricately woven into the fabric of meat dependency. Meanwhile, two thirds of the world's oceans tremble on the brink of ecological collapse due almost entirely to commercial fishing.

The West has developed a meat culture which reaches its zenith in the USA but has also spread throughout Europe and is now infecting virtually the whole of the globe. It is a diet which requires almost 40 per cent of the world's grain harvest to be fed to animals,[1] inefficiently converting 10 kilograms of vegetable protein into only one kilogram of meat.[2] It is a diet which uses four and a half times more land than is necessary for a strictly plant-based diet – two and a quarter more than for a vegetarian diet.[3] Because of our complete control over the economies of developing countries we require them to produce fodder to feed our animals while their children starve to death. Meat is intimately linked with famine and starvation. Through the stranglehold of the World Bank and International Monetary Fund we impose both our philosophy and our economics on cultures which have survived for centuries, legitimizing greed and destruction.

There could, perhaps, be some remote justification for all this if meat were an essential part of our diet and necessary for our development. But the reverse is true. Much as we might find it difficult to acknowledge, we are primates, closely related to the great apes. Like them, our teeth, hands, toes, gut and digestive processes are those of a fruit eater, a herbivore, designed to cope with nuts, seeds and plants.

In fact the rapid increase in meat consumption since the Second World War has seriously damaged our health. Despite all the doom-laden caution about vegetarianism, vegetarians live longer and suffer less from a whole range of diseases. Every major survey confirms this. The major killer in the West is heart disease and vegetarians are up to 50 per cent less likely to die of it.[4] Cancer is the second biggest killer and vegetarians stand up to 50 per cent less risk of developing any kind of cancer.[5] Two of the essential elements recently found to preserve human health – dietary fibre[6] and antioxidants[7] – are not present in meat.

Meanwhile pigs are tethered in barren stalls, so deprived of stimulation that they frequently go mad. Calves only days old are separated from their mothers, transported to crates where they can barely move and are purposely made anaemic in solitary confinement. Chickens, naturally restless, strutting creatures, are crammed five to a wire cage little bigger than a microwave oven.

It all culminates in the barbarity of slaughter where cruelty is casually dispensed on a unimaginable scale – spinal columns of conscious sheep severed with the probings of a domestic screwdriver; paralysed bullocks urged to stand with 70,000 volt shocks to the testicles; fully conscious lambs slashed across the throat because time is of the essence. In all, more than 750 million animals are slaughtered in Britain every year in a production line of destructive misery.[8] The casual indifference towards the suffering of creatures brutalizes those who carry it out and those who allow it to happen in their name. It denies all our claims of being civilized.

Throughout this book I know I am going to be accused of anthropomorphism, but that's much too easy and not accurate. I do, I admit, adore animals and the natural world and I am fascinated by the amazing adaptability of nature, in particular how animals have reached such perfection in their own sphere. To me it is self-evident that their lives are equally as important to them as ours are to us.

We kid ourselves about the extent of our knowledge, pretending we have reached a peak of understanding, arrived at through superior intellect, but the truth is much more prosaic, much less complacent. The Earth has existed for nearly five billion years, during which time various life forms have developed and evolved. One common thread runs through this extraordinary phenomenon and that is the ability of individual species to live within their environment, part of it and dependent upon it. In evolutionary terms human beings have been here for little more than a twinkling of light. But already we have begun to tear and break the individual strands which go to make up this fine web of existence.

Modern Western teaching, both political and religious, places us above and beyond the rules by which all other animals live, as though they simply don't apply to us, as though we are not animals ourselves. As a species we have looked at the world and said that nothing matters but us and all its glories are there to be exploited – and if they can't be exploited then they count for very little. We destroy without knowing the long-term effects of such actions and even when we do know, we continue to destroy because today is much more important than tomorrow. It is by today's achievements, today's boasts, today's profit margins that we are judged.

As a consequence, Governments look at the problems which

surround us and are frozen into immobility. They must know that the only effective cure is an approach to life based on co-operation and concern, on conservation rather than consumption, on real education rather than exam-passing. But they can do nothing because such a philosophy threatens the ethos which grants them power, wealth and influence. The very ethos which has brought the planet teetering to the edge of environmental destruction is, we are told, the same philosophy which will save us.

So every supposed environmental agreement, whether to limit fishing or reduce logging, is quickly ignored in the scramble to make money. When it comes to a choice between preservation and destruction, if the short-term interests of multinational corporations are involved it is invariably the latter which triumphs. We know, for instance, that smoking is the biggest avoidable killer and yet every high street is littered with advertisements for cigarettes and we even spread the contamination to the developing countries. We know that a vegetarian diet is much healthier than a meat-based diet and yet it is the livestock farmers and the cattle feed farmers who receive most of the Government subsidies. We know that poverty destroys people, but the gap between rich and poor constantly grows wider. Knowledge and understanding have ceased to be signposts to the future and have become minor obstacles to be circumvented in the quest for profit.

As a species we have set ourselves up as the arbiters of the globe in an act of such breathtaking arrogance that it usurps the role of gods and creates a monstrous imbalance in the natural order. We slaughter owls, hawks, crows and magpies so that grouse or pheasants can be reared in large numbers. We then slaughter them by sending lead shot ripping through their flesh – and call it sport. We destroy rabbits as vermin and then demonize the foxes which live on them. We then hunt the foxes.

We gas badgers because they might have TB; we trap and kill rooks because we don't like their habits; chase hares with dogs for entertainment; do anything we like to rats and mice; shoot pigeons in their tens of thousands. We determine which animals we will eat and deny them everything; we determine which will be labelled vermin and try to annihilate them; we allow others the comfort of our hearth. Across the globe we chase whales and harpoon them for cultural reasons. We destroy dolphins and seals because they dare to eat fish. There is hardly a species which we will not exterminate if their interests and ours collide.

By selective breeding, genetic manipulation and dietary interference we are also producing food animals which are increasingly incapable of life without our intervention. As factory farming intensifies so medical intervention with antibiotics and other powerful drugs increases and alongside the increase goes a resistance to the very drugs vital to the animals' survival. We are producing animals with a tenuous grip on life and at the same time are destroying the wild gene pool from which they evolved.

By so cavalierly playing with the fate of other animals we are risking our own. It seems we are incapable of understanding that every living creature has its part to play in maintaining the glorious fabric of our world. None of the animals which we slaughter, even those we demonize as vermin, pose any threat to the survival of the planet. It is not they which threaten its existence but us.

The only hope we have is to fundamentally reassess our role and our attitude to the planet and the living creatures which share it with us. When a calf is prodded and dragged into the killing pen, wide-eyed and terrified, with the stench of blood and death in its nostrils, we are all demeaned. When the captive bolt shatters its forehead, there is no compassion. When the slaughterer's hand grabs the muzzle of a lamb to stifle its bleating and applies the knife to its throat, there is no compassion. And without compassion there is little hope for any of us.

What is the first step? Vegetarianism is one of the few individual acts you can perform that has an immediate impact. It is the first step in ending the daily cruelties handed out to farm animals. It is the first step in allowing the planet to heal itself. But it is much more than all of these. It is a political act and a clear expression of a belief in a different way of doing things, a different kind of world – a better world.

One by one we are extinguishing the voices which fill this ark in space. For all we know it may be the only ark in space. Those voices that can still be heard, including the human ones, are increasingly sounding stressed and tortured. Unless there are dramatic changes in the way we live our lives, it will become a totally silent ark.

1 ◆ THROUGH THE EYES OF A PIG

I was 15 years old when I decided to become a vegetarian. It wasn't the outcome of argument or debate, or the process of intellectual investigation, not to begin with at any rate. It was because of a look.

A student friend was working on an agricultural project and needed to visit a model farm. I went along for the ride. If I was naïve to think that hens would be strutting and scratching around a farmyard, all glistening feathers and clucking contentment, then I was not alone. The veil of silence which surrounded animal production then, in 1979 – and which still does – had simply not prepared me for what I saw.

My vague notions of stack yards, scattered straw and wandering animals disappeared instantly. There were no animals to be seen, only a collection of ugly, windowless, industrial buildings which could just as easily have been do-it-yourself stores or engineering workshops.

We started in the pig house. As soon as I walked through the door, into an atmosphere cloyingly warm and damp and laced with the smells of 100 defecating pigs, the first nagging unease began to gnaw at me. There were no cosy sties, no wallowing contentment, just row upon row of individual concrete stalls, each pig separated from its neighbours, unable to touch them despite being only centimetres away.

These pigs, I was informed, were the breeding stock, the pregnant sows who would provide two and a half litters of piglets every year, each litter frequently running to double figures. Ahead of each creature was nothing but iron bars to which were clipped feeding troughs. Beneath their feet was slatted metal through which most of their excreta would hopefully drop. However, when they urinated it splashed up from the floor, wetting the sides of the stall and the pigs' legs and belly. They would eventually lie down in it. I noticed that any movement tended to result in a scrabble to maintain a firm footing.

Around the middle of each sow was a broad collar with an attached shackle, securing her to the ground. With this restraint she could take little more than half a pace forward and half a pace back. Those sows who tried to lie down did so with difficulty.

When confronted with horror of this kind, there is always a tendency to explain it away, to excuse it, to want to believe that it cannot possibly be as bad for the animal as it appears. We're encouraged in this. 'Give them warmth, food and water and they're as happy as Larry,' grinned our guide. I didn't believe it.

In fact years later I was to watch as a young sow was placed in a stall for the first time. As the tether was attached around her middle and the shackle secured to the floor, she threw herself against the restraint in a frenzy of squealing and panic.

At the farm I visited, the poor creatures had given up the fruitless struggle of resistance. They had no option. The effect of their barren and sterile existence was obvious to see. Many of them exhibited a syndrome known as 'stereotypic behaviour', moving their heads backwards and forwards in an exact and constantly repeated motion, gnawing on their bars in a particular and regular way with the precision of a metronome.

It is the same syndrome which causes zoo animals to pace backwards and forwards relentlessly, and as the Government-supported CRB Research states in a review of the scientific evidence of the welfare of pigs, this behaviour 'resembles in many respects the development in humans of chronic psychiatric disorders'.[1] Many of the pigs I was looking at had quite literally gone mad.

As I stood there and watched the sows in their endless boredom, I could appreciate what a superb example it presented of accountancy and veterinary skills combining together to reduce waste, to maximize profit, optimize food intake and reduce staffing. In the planning, design and construction of this model plant every question had been asked and answered except one: what about the animals?

Pigs are highly intelligent animals, descendants of the wild pigs which once roamed Britain's forests until they were hunted to extinction in the seventeenth century. In their natural state they would have wandered the great woods that covered most of these islands, eating beech nuts and acorns, seeds and roots and occasionally small mammals, rooting them out with their strong snouts and necks. Not keen on temperature extremes, they would seek shade under the trees when it became too hot and would build nests from the leaf litter to keep them warm in winter.

For creatures with such a strong sense of community, active and sociable, the decision to imprison them in solitary and idle confinement denies them even a semblance of their natural existence. Such a policy reflects our greed and lack of compassion. Pigs have become a product, have been manipulated and specially bred to produce particular types of meat. Ones with especially long backs produce more bacon rashers; ones with sturdy hocks produce better hams. The dominance of money, the logic of efficiency, the adulation of profit are epitomized in the pig-breeding shed.

The sows remain in their pens, known as 'dry-sow stalls', for most of their 16½-week pregnancy and the only remission from the boredom is to be moved to a farrowing crate as they approach full term.

These crates, little bigger than the dry-sow stalls, were in an adjoining building and we were proudly shown them by our guide. I was bemused by the actions of one heavily pregnant pig. In her barren, slatted, metal-floored prison she moved relentlessly backwards and forwards as though desperately looking for something when there was obviously nothing to find. I asked what she was doing and the question was casually dismissed. I found out later. It was another example of stereo-typic behaviour, another indication of the animal's mental collapse.

Sows have extremely strong maternal feelings and in the wild would begin building a huge nest many days before they were due to farrow. When completed it could be as much as one metre high. Their search for leaves and twigs and straw might well take them on a journey of several kilometres. What I had witnessed was the pathetic actions of a pregnant female trying to fulfil her natural instincts in a totally barren environment.

In other crates, other sows had already given birth. Little piglets, still wet and smeared with mucus, scrabbled on the metal floor to find their mother's teats. In one crate, they struggled pathetically to climb the inclined floor, negotiating a route past a dead sibling and the discarded placenta. The mother could do nothing to assist as she was restrained by a series of bars which allowed her young to suckle but prevented her from playing any maternal role other than that of milk provider. 'The bars? Stops the sow from rolling on her young,' explained our smiling guide.

By now it was a smile I had grown to despise. This grinning, grimacing young man, little older than me, spoke fluently and passionately of increased yields, boasted knowledgeably about feed ratios and spoke reverentially of market demands. Not once did a solitary word of concern or an expression of interest in the animals around us escape his lips other than in their role as economic units. I knew nothing about pigs before I entered those sheds but I knew that what I was looking at was a betrayal of simple humanity.

Our guided tour continued on its way, into the rearing section of the same shed. Thousands of bright little eyes atop constantly twitching snouts watched us from minuscule prisons wherever we went. Tiers of stacked, slatted boxes, one on top of another up to a height of about two metres, flanked the aisle. Each 'piggi-box' contained several piglets, each box was totally devoid of any material item, each box had become home to its occupants when they were three-and-a-half weeks old and were removed from their mother – some five weeks earlier than would naturally be the case.

Their lives would be extremely short. Those selected for ham and pork would be killed at about five months old. Those to be used for bacon might survive an additional month. Both varieties would be removed from the boxes and crammed into fattening pens a few weeks before their slaughter. Nervous and extraordinarily jumpy, they would live there on a bare floor without any bedding, without trees or flowers or sunlight.

Pork now accounts for 40 per cent of global meat production.[2] Pigs are eaten more frequently than any other animal and are intensively farmed throughout the world. In the USA in the 1960s, 'Bacon Bins' were developed, where piglets are kept individually in bare cages, also so small that they can hardly move.[3] This stops the piglets 'wasting' energy on exercise, making them 'get fat quick'.

Such treatment of animals is always excused as being in their best interests. Those who work with them claim to know and understand their habits and dismiss concerns from people such as me with complete contempt. They maintain that so long as an animal is provided with food and water and shelter from the elements, it will want nothing else. It's extraordinary that they can be so dismissive of freedom, a concept which we, as human animals, value above all else. Freedom fires the imagination with its vision and depresses the soul with its absence. I believe it is the same for all animals. If you doubt me, watch a herd of cows as they're released from their cramped winter sheds onto the fresh grass of spring.

At 15, I saw things which I instinctively knew were wrong but I was unable to rationalize them, was incapable of mounting an argument against the bland persuasions of my guide. So I was determined to begin the search for information as soon as I left that oppressive animal prison. I was sickened at what I discovered.

Left to mature naturally, suckled by their mothers in open surroundings, piglets scamper and chase, tumble over each other and play the energetic learning games that occupy all young mammals. They do not damage each other. They exhibit all the same antics we love in our own pets. Crammed together in their boxes, commercial piglets can do none of these things and so their curiosity turns inwards. The stultifying boredom produces what the breeders accusingly call 'vices', such as severely biting each other's tails, or even cannibalism. You don't have to be selected for *University Challenge* to work out that one possible cure is to allow them more space and some stimulation which will give their curiosity the full rein it needs. But that, of course, is uneconomic.

How the breeders answer the problem is to 'dock' their tails.

That innocuous-sounding little word, like 'cull' for kill or 'geld' for castrate, gives no indication of its reality – slicing through the tail, either all or part, with a knife but without anaesthetic. Other farmers have a different solution, one sometimes used in combination with docking. They remove the piglets' teeth with pliers…

Our guide ignored these mutilations and proudly boasted that when the pigs go to slaughter every part of their anatomy is used – everything but the squeal.

Still smiling, he led us back into the area of the dry-sow stalls, again boasting of the pig unit's modern techniques which maximized production to the optimum. Five days after the young piglets are removed from their mothers, the sows are made pregnant again and the misery-go-round continues.

As he spoke we passed a strange-looking device, a kind of low block with straps on it. I asked what it was. 'Oh, this is what the bunny lovers call the "rape rack",' he chuckled.

This little device is designed to hold a sow immobile while she is impregnated by one of the breeding boars. Pigs are naturally choosy about their mates, but here there was no selection, no right of refusal, just an endless cycle of pregnancy, farrowing, separation from the offspring and pregnancy again. When they are finally exhausted by this existence and their piglet yield drops or their body tissues break down into tumours and abscesses, these baby machines face an ironic destiny. Their slaughtered carcasses are used in the processed food industry for pies, sausages – and baby food.

Up to this point in my life I had perceived animal cruelty to be such things as fox hunting, seal culling or the abuse of domestic pets by their owners. In fact the most serious confrontation I had ever had with my father – a bitter, shouting, angry scene – was when I took the money he'd given me for a haircut and sent it to the campaign to end the clubbing of baby seals on Canada's ice floes. I returned home still with my hair but proud of myself. I couldn't understand why he was so angry. I still can't. When the seal trade was finally banned, I didn't hesitate to remind him of my, and his, role in it. He still refers to it. However, we were both horrified when in 1996 the Canadian Government announced it was to restart this barbaric practice and authorized the killing of 250,000 seals.

My visit to this model farm was beginning to challenge all my perceptions. I kept asking myself why I had never been told about the way farm animals are treated. I had been reared, as children still are, on a romantic myth of contented cows called Daisy and Buttercup and smiling sows called Mrs Pig.

The farm was not even some isolated aberration but a show-piece. It was an example for farmers to follow. Its methods and practices constituted the industry's recommended pig management and production techniques and provided all the necessary information on how to maximize output, contain costs and make more money from the animals. And in the 1990s, with our consumerist, capitalist model an example for the developing world, the export of factory-farming units and their associated technology is a boom industry.

Today in Britain over 800,000 sows are kept for breeding, half of them in dry-sow stalls. Most of the remainder live in high density units where they are spared the sterility of solitary confinement but where the space available is still extremely restricted.

In 1991, Sir Richard Body, a Conservative MP, introduced a Parliamentary Bill to outlaw dry-sow stalls and tethers. Had the Bill progressed, they would already be a part of our shameful history, just like bear baiting or cock fighting. However, one of his parliamentary colleagues undertook to 'talk it out' – in the interests of the farming industry's profitability, you understand.

Talking out is a cynical abuse of parliamentary procedures where a politician, either individually or in concert with others, can stand up in the House and talk utter nonsense for as long as they can manage it. If they go on long enough, the Bill fails because there is insufficient time left to take a vote. ('What did you do today, dear?' 'Talked complete and utter bollocks for five and a half hours so that 400,000 pregnant sows can continue to be strapped to the floor for another seven years. Pass the canapés!')

A compromise Bill did go through, outlawing the system in 1998. But the decision applies only to the UK. We will continue to import thousands of tonnes of pig meat and bacon from countries like Holland and Denmark which will continue with sow stalls, as will the USA, where pig farms have become huge industrial complexes, confining millions of sows in narrow steel prisons.

Back in the pig-breeding shed, the final act in my disturbing drama came at the end of the rows of sow stalls where a few separate, only slightly larger pens were set aside from the rest. In each one was a huge boar, the missing players in this carefully constructed reproductive production line. The one nearest to me stood motionless, his huge head hanging low towards the barren floor. As I came level with him he raised his head and dragged himself slowly towards me on lame legs. With deliberation he looked straight at me, staring directly into my eyes.

It seemed to me that I saw in those sad, intelligent, penetrating eyes a plea, a question to which I had no answer: 'Why are you doing this to me?' Without embarrassment or shame I burst into tears, silent sobs shaking my body, and I kept repeating over and over: 'I'm sorry, I'm so sorry.'

It was an emotional response but that emotion has not diminished with age. I can recall it whenever I choose. If ever I need a reminder, that sad and accusing boar is there to motivate me and to encourage me.

Of course my age at that time put me in that group which is constantly described as 'vulnerable', 'impressionable' or even 'over-emotional'. It is this same age group that I now spend much of my time talking to in schools across the country. Their enthusiasm and clear untrammelled view of what constitutes cruelty is not only refreshing, it's what keeps me going. You may call it 'emotion', I call it 'compassion'.

Young people believe they can change the world and who are we to tell them they can't? I remember that feeling so well. With my pig experience and other newly discovered information I honestly believed that all I had to do to stop people eating meat was to tell them the truth. I was staggered when it had no effect on my family. They didn't know it then, but we were engaged in a battle of attrition which was to last for years. There would be individual skirmishes, guerrilla tactics and confrontational arguments. 'Oh my God, you're not eating that are you?' I would exclaim, as a forkful of meat hesitated on my mother's lips. Every meat-containing package in the fridge and freezer was embellished with a 'This Package Contains a Dead Animal' sticker.

My mother listened to my arguments and never shouted at me or battled with me. But I don't think she fully understood the depth of my feelings or truly believed the things I told her. I think her main concern was for my health and so at first she retaliated with what I can only describe as underhand methods. Suddenly I was confronted with numerous rice dishes and always lurking amongst the peppers and onions were indeterminate little pieces of something, usually chicken. I think I always detected them.

I kept to my beliefs and was determined to educate my parents. After a while my mother accepted my views and became fully supportive. Now, my sister and brother are vegetarian while my father, in typical male fashion, accepts the arguments but is slow to change. But I count this outcome as a partial victory.

The most frustrating aspect of my attempts to convert them was when I was unable to answer their arguments in favour of meat eating. I instinctively knew that I was listening to regurgitations of old wives' tales, myths and half truths. But I had nothing with which to counter them. I set about remedying that.

2 ◆ THE CHICKEN AND THE EGG

Home economics, now appropriately renamed 'food technology', was never one of my favourite subjects. However, it was through this that at the age of 16 I was allowed to go on a guided tour of an egg, chicken rearing and processing plant. That simple statement sounds innocuous, but it isn't how I felt. I had made a decision never again to eat meat because I no longer wanted animals to suffer and be killed in my name. I had never seen an animal killed and the thought of it was abhorrent to me, but here I was, about to witness just that, entirely of my own volition.

My family had never witnessed slaughter either. No one I knew had ever seen it. In fact very few meat eaters have. I found it extraordinary that people should be so protected from the source of their food. Now I'm quite happy to show a carrot seed being planted and the grown root being dug up, washed and chopped into pieces. The only part I draw the line at is demonstrating it being cooked, because that would expose how bad I am at it! Meat eaters, on the other hand, are precious beyond belief about the source of their food. If the whole process of transport, stunning, slaughter and butchery is so natural to us, why do parents go to such lengths to protect their children from witnessing these things?

It was with great apprehension that I arrived at yet another soulless, windowless, undistinguished building – a battery hen house in the rural beauty of the Lancashire countryside. The overriding impression was one of ugliness and protruding from the roof were the rows of little round ventilators which have become synonymous with battery egg production. Almost anywhere in Europe, and possibly now anywhere in the world, you are likely to be confronted by them, often in the most idyllic setting.

My guide opened the door and asked me to enter quickly. 'The air pressure inside the building is slightly higher than outside. It keeps the ammonia down.'

I must have been too slow because as I walked inside, the overpowering stench of ammonia took my breath away. So powerful was it that I had an almost instant headache and it was several seconds before I was conscious of the noise – 15,000 clucking, squawking hens, an incessant, throbbing, burbling sound which continues in such places for 17 hours a day. This artificially lit, constantly long day is totally independent of the rising and setting of the sun and is designed to extract the maximum number of eggs from the chickens.

This was a comparatively small battery and many are now twice this size. But even so, the tiers of cages, four deep, ranked on either side of the aisle, filled every available space. There were several aisles, each flanked by a similar number of cages. I walked up and down them, my ears filled with the babble of hens, my nose assailed by the stench of ammonia, my vision limited by the partial light. I was deaf to the running commentary of my guide.

One simple fact illustrates the space allotted to each bird. A fully grown hen, which all of these were, has a wing span of about 76 cm. Each cage was only 50 cm wide and 45 cm deep, only a fraction bigger than the average family microwave oven.

For the 18 months to two years that each bird spends inside her cage, she can never spread her wings to their full extent. Even more disturbing is the fact that each bird shares this minimal space with four others.

As if to confirm that they were no longer seen as sentient creatures, these chickens, I was informed, were 579s. They were not even dignified with a name.

Their condition was sadly pathetic. Most had great patches of feathers missing and some were nearly bald. Food and water were dispensed from automatic troughs in front of the cages. Any movement by a bird, whether to eat, drink, change her position or avoid being pecked, required her to push and shove or clamber over her cage mates.

I noticed that the end of each bird's beak was missing, as though the last few millimetres had simply been sliced away. I was later to discover that this is precisely what had happened. At a few days old, many of the chicks destined to be placed in battery cages have their beaks thrust into the red-hot blades of a beak-trimming machine. With exact precision, it severs part of the beak, theoretically cauterizing it at the same time.

There is something particularly pathetic about little bewildered chicks, blinking erratically while droplets of blood ooze from the end of their severed beaks. Many die from the shock and others simply bleed to death.

For years we've been led to believe that the beak is a piece of unfeeling, dead tissue but recent research by Michael Gentle and colleagues at the Institute of Animal Physiology and Genetics Research in Edinburgh has challenged that, making the practice of debeaking even more disturbing. The beak is, in fact, a complex and sensitive organ containing an extensive nerve supply. The pain which results, according to Gentle *et al.*, causes 'long-term chronic pain and depression' and may be felt by the bird for its entire life.[1]

I was to discover that other, even less attractive practices are necessary to keep the battery system operating. These include adding a slosh of antibiotics to try and control disease, and feeding their own dead and even their own excreta back to the hens as food supplements to control costs and 'stay competitive'. This, of course, is the ideal way to ensure that diseases become endemic.

That explanation that animals need only food and shelter to be content is matched by the second most common palliative – only happy animals breed in captivity. Battery chickens, of course, don't breed because they never see a cockerel and their eggs are therefore infertile, but they do lay a lot of eggs, on average some 300 a year, compared with their wild counterparts' 10 or 12, and this egg-laying process is trumpeted as a sign of their contentment. Ironically, it provides probably the hens' greatest cause of stress. The cages they inhabit consist of nothing but wire bars – floor, ceiling and sides. So they have no choice other than to be in constant bodily contact with each other. For both their wild ancestors and even their farmyard cousins, egg laying is an extremely private, even solitary affair. The process can take up to an hour and the laying hen will always remove herself from the rest of the flock before beginning it.

Perhaps it's as well I was unaware of this as I slowly walked down aisle after aisle of caged chickens. Of course I could see them jostling each other, but had no idea that those about to lay were trying to hide from the others, climbing beneath them to seek privacy and solitude. Hide? It's like a person attempting to conceal themselves from four others in the same telephone box.

As they finally laid their eggs, each one rolled across the wire mesh floor and plopped into a small conveyor belt at the back of the cage, where it was carried away to be washed and packed.

And this is where marketing comes cynically into its own.

Television advertising assails us with images of chickens who cluck happily and trot eagerly to their deaths. Their eggs, produced in totally artificial light, the result of an unnatural, often cannibalistic diet in an environment akin to a breakers' yard, are sweetly termed 'country fresh' or 'farm fresh'. The boxes are adorned with pictures of wheat ears and sometimes even thatched cottages. That's marketing for you!

Of course certain facts are never mentioned – the tonnes of faeces which drop down through the cages, from one bird onto another, before finally settling on the floor of the battery; the brittle, broken bones, resulting from a calcium deficient diet and lack of exercise, which affect one third of the 35 million battery hens alive in Britain at any given time, rising to over 90 per cent by the time they're slaughtered.[2] If these facts were known, it is unlikely that battery eggs would account for the 85 to 90 per cent of all egg sales in Britain, the rest of Europe and the USA which they did in 1995.[3]

It's difficult to contemplate the degree of suffering which must be experienced by the millions of chickens who spend their days and nights with broken bones, unable ever to rest properly or to find a position which mitigates the pain. If you ever needed any confirmation that this hurts then Edinburgh University can supply it. As a result of their 1991 review of all scientific studies on battery farming they came to the conclusion that battery hens do suffer.[4] You could never work that one out without a science degree, could you? However, they did go on to say that the battery system should be outlawed. They are not the first to do so.

But the cruelty continues unabated. Even as the Edinburgh study was completed, on a site designated as 'a special landscape area', Corby Borough Council granted permission to the Plymouth-based Horizon Poultry Farms to build the largest battery hen unit in the whole of Europe and MAFF gave a grant of £50,000 and made a recommendation to the EC that Horizon should receive a further £200,000 from the agricultural fund. In a piece of manoeuvring, the money was cleverly ear-marked for the egg-packing plant and not for the caging of the 1,600,000 hens. This cleared MAFF of any charge of abusing animals. What the money was actually used for is merely semantics, however, because without this and the other financial inducements the project may have been economically unviable.

Any arguments against such use of public money are usually countered with the response that new jobs will be created. If you question the lack of morality you are normally dismissed as having misguided sentiment which places concern for animals above concern for humans. However, concern for employment is cynically inconsistent. Miners, steel workers and shipbuilders don't merit any Government subsidy and hundreds of thousands were thrown out of work during the 1980s while nuclear power workers, fishermen and livestock farmers (not vegetable farmers, mark you) merited subsidy. Would it be too simplistic or cynical to suggest that there aren't a lot of votes to be gained from coal miners or steel workers or shipbuilders who tend to be of a different political persuasion from the Conservative party?

It is important to be absolutely clear what happens in the name of subsidy, for which you pay through the tax deducted from your earnings.

For every chicken in a battery cage, another chicken has been killed. The stumbling block is that the breeding hens from which battery chickens are obtained tend to produce an equal number of male and female chicks. The females have been specially bred to produce as many eggs as possible but to be low in body weight, scrawny, in order to keep feed consumption to a minimum. However, the scrawniness also affects male chicks so they're not suitable for meat. They can't lay eggs either. In fact they're no good for anything at all, not even life.

At a day old, the newly hatched chicks are sexed by an experienced chicken sexer – females this side, males that. The females are boxed up and despatched to cages to be grown on, where they will stay until transferred to battery cages at about 18 weeks old. There they will stay until their egg laying begins to drop off, usually at between 18 months and two years old. As soon as that happens they're slaughtered and used for soups, pastes, stock cubes, the restaurant trade, baby foods and even school meals. Creatures that would naturally live a minimum of seven years are considered redundant at only two and for almost the whole of that period are denied the ability to fulfil even their most basic instincts.

The male chicks are unceremoniously dumped into a bin. When it's full, with hundreds of chicks piled one on top of the other, the ones at the bottom struggling to get to the top, the bin is transferred either to the carbon dioxide gas chamber or the crusher, depending on the preference of the particular producer. The fate of these tiny creatures is to be fed to other captive animals, to be turned into fertilizer or processed into chicken and other feed. The scale of this slaughter is breathtaking – according to MAFF, 40 million day-old chicks every year.[5]

There are numerous eyewitness accounts of still living chicks struggling beneath the weight of their dead companions as they emerge from the gas chambers. One can only guess at their eventual fate.

Of course, MAFF has a clear view on this carnage: 'We definitely recommend the use of one hundred per cent carbon dioxide gas.'[6]

The constant drive to intensify all livestock production and to increase the amount of animal products in the national diet began after the Second World War and has now reached a

frenzy. It has nothing to do with nutrition or need but is based
on the financial return available on invested capital. For people
with money to invest, livestock rearing is no different from a
bank or building society. All the investor wants to know is how
much interest they will make. If chickens cease to be profitable,
the money will be moved into tobacco or armaments or motor
cars. To ensure the investors stay happy, breeders will do almost
anything to keep their profitability as high as possible. And that
means pushing animals beyond their ability to cope. They are
simply units of production. The truth is that capitalism knows
absolutely no morality and the only thing which brings about
change is public pressure.

As I continued my tour, I understood perfectly why people
would want to demonstrate and shout and make an apathetic
public listen. The denial of any rights to living, feeling creatures
was beyond my comprehension. But as I walked through the
dim light of the battery sheds and the stench of ammonia, I
was already beginning to learn political skills. I didn't shout or
argue with my guide, but was determined to speak to the man
responsible. It was easier than I thought.

The owner was a middle-aged man dressed in typical
farmer's gear, polite and composed. He outlined the history
of his farm and explained that although the battery I had just
seen contained 15,000 birds, the total number at the farm was
200,000. Then, in a bizarre twist, he struck a censorial stance
and spoke about Continental producers as having much larger
batteries, as though the scale of the operation were the concern,
not the system itself.

'I love chickens,' he insisted, 'and everything I do here is in
the best interests of the birds.' I was about to have my first lesson
in the use of statistics. 'Free range chickens are much worse off.
Not only have they got to be debeaked because they peck each

other, but they get more diseases. The whole environment here is carefully worked out to control this. Even the dimmed light is to the benefit of the hens. Listen, I don't want chickens dying because that's just money down the drain and there's a 3 per cent lower mortality amongst battery hens than free range.'

I instinctively knew I was being misled – and so I was. The comparison he was using was that of high density birds which can be crammed 2,000 or 3,000 to a shed but because they have access to a bit of outside land are termed 'free range'. Under these circumstances their whole social order breaks down and many hens won't risk venturing out in case they have to cross another bird's territory or because of congestion at the exits and entrances. The land outside the shed becomes saturated with droppings and poisoned and it is this which accounts for the increased mortality.

Way back in 1948, L. F. Easterbrook wrote in *Picture Post*:

> But can it be really true that birds kept under these unnatural conditions, without exercise, without exposure to the sun and the wind and the rain, so debilitated that they are admittedly unfit for breeding, often with their bones so brittle that they snap like dry twigs – can it be really true that the eggs they produce for us are just as nourishing as eggs from birds kept very differently?

The brittle bones that he wrote about are a direct consequence of the hens being forced to produce such an unnatural quantity of eggs in restricted conditions. Each eggshell uses up two and a half grams of calcium, almost 10 per cent of the hen's normal body reserves. Over the course of a year and 300 eggs, a hen will use 25 times the normal amount of calcium in her body.[7] The result is osteoporosis. The bones waste and become weak and it takes very little for them to break. This disease affects almost all laying hens.

But that isn't the end of their problems. Other common diseases are prolapses, egg peritonitis, infectious bronchitis and 'cage layer fatigue', a form of paralysis. There is also a rapidly increasing threat from Gumboro disease, a viral cancer, and on top of that, avian leukosis, the bird variety of leukaemia, is now commonplace.

An infinitely better way of producing eggs is in small-scale, free range flocks of about 100, not the 400 birds to the acre recommended by the EC. In these smaller numbers, the birds can organize their social order without too much stress. But it is important to remember that the male of the species is still killed at a day old, whether free range or battery.

Anyone who believes that chickens do not suffer from being forced into a cage in which they spend their whole lives standing or squatting on wire mesh should watch a genuinely free range bird and its habits. Given the opportunity, it will cover a huge area, even several acres. In extreme heat it will sit quietly in the shade, but for the rest of the day it will wander about ceaselessly, using its powerful feet and legs to look for bugs and beetles, seeds and grains. It will strut and stride, pushing the grass aside with powerful thrusts of its feet, watching carefully to see what it has unearthed. It will find a dusty piece of land in which to bathe and throw dust everywhere with apparent pleasure and enthusiasm. You don't need to know that it has a large brain for the size of its body because its intelligence is obvious. It is an irony that these egg-laying machines never have the opportunity to mother because they are extremely careful and protective towards their young.

For me, one of the inhuman acts which encapsulates so much of what threatens this world is our treatment of birds. Since humans could first express their thoughts they have watched birds with fascination and envy. Their ability to soar into the sky, to hang almost motionless on a rising thermal, to look down and see the world as we could only hope to see it, has entranced and captivated us.

And what have we done to the creatures with this wonderful freedom? We have taken parrots, as gregarious, noisy and boisterous as a teenage party, locked them in solitary confinement and boasted when we have taught them to say 'Pretty Polly'. We have taken linnets from the tree tops, blinded them and left them to sing their hearts out in lonely darkness. We have taken descendants of the jungle fowl, who criss-cross the forests in restless search, and have crammed them five to a cage. And in cynical deception, we tell the world that they prefer it that way.

3 ◆ THE SIX-WEEK LIFECYCLE

A measure of how much public opinion has shifted in a comparatively short time is the attitude of factory farmers to their livelihood. Sixteen years ago, at the time of my first school tour around the farm units, they showed no embarrassment or guilt, and secrecy and defensiveness were only a small part of their armoury. Try ringing your local neighbourhood broiler farm today to request a conducted tour and see what response you get. Saddam Hussein would stand a better chance of being the keynote speaker at a Tory party conference. However, at the time I was first shown around the battery sheds, attitudes were still comparatively open.

The idea of intensive production began, as already mentioned, after the Second World War and in the following years the mechanics of automation were perfected – automated feeding systems, egg collection techniques, mechanically assisted lay ratios and the optimum heat and light levels. I find it extremely difficult to comprehend how the concepts of a Ford production line could be applied to breathing, living creatures, but they are.

Broiler chickens (kept for meat, not eggs) are subjected to the same concept of efficiency as battery hens, with no less impoverished results. As if to distance themselves from the biological reality of what they do, chicken farmers refer to themselves as 'growers' and the chickens as a 'crop'. This kind of thinking is pernicious. It reached a high point during an interview I did in 1991, during the launch of my campaign, 'Feeding You the Facts', on ITV's lunchtime news with the Director of the Meat and Livestock Commission. To my complete disbelief he said that chickens weren't animals. Then, with a little help from me, he nearly drowned in his own embarrassment.

Anyway, back on the 'home economics' tour, once I had finished with the battery hen house, I was proudly given the full tour of the chicken crop. What I am going to describe is typical of the dozens of broiler units that I have subsequently visited over the past decade. We started with a newly stocked broiler shed filled with chicks no more than few days old. The scale of the operation was staggering. The building itself was similar to all modern agricultural structures – windowless, soulless and airless. The floor was covered with a thick layer of litter which looked like a combination of wood shavings, saw dust and chopped straw. It still had that fresh, strong and pleasant odour of outdoors – part timber yard, part stack yard.

Running from end to end of the shed, across the floor and equidistant from each other, were three automated feeding lines, each conveyor carrying a slowly moving cargo of high-protein food pellets through the myriad of yellow chicks which carpeted the floor. The air was filled with their high-pitched tweetings as they wandered around, from conveyor belt to water dispenser and back again.

There were 20,000 of them under this one roof but other sheds contained as many as 100,000. Although crowded, there was sufficient room for them to move around. Perhaps they felt nothing about their situation, perhaps they were quite happy in their thousands, but watching a clutch of chicks with their mother in natural surroundings, you are conscious of a very different kind of life.

The second shed I was shown into presented an entirely different scene. It was identical in structure to the first one but the floor was almost completely taken up with full-grown chickens and the light was significantly dimmer. In only six weeks, the 20,000 little chicks had been transformed into 'fully-grown birds with a live weight of 1.8 kg – ideal for the dining table'. And that's where they were headed the next day.

As I looked around at the milling mass in its almost perm-anent twilight, each bird allocated a space smaller than the area taken up by a telephone directory, I felt there was something wrong. I couldn't identify what it was at first but then realized it had to do with the noise. It was only when I thought back to the sounds that battery chickens make, that squawking, clucking, all-pervasive, never-ending burble, that the answer came to me. I was looking at a carpet of fat, fully-grown chickens but I was listening to the high-pitched tweet of chicks. Had I known it, their eyes would have told the same story – they were the bright blue colour of immaturity rather than the almost jet-like darkness of adulthood.

The reasons for this were provided spontaneously and proudly by my guide. A process of selective breeding and dietary control has produced a bird which grows twice as quickly as it did only 25 or 30 years ago. Working on the basis that the more a bird can be encouraged to eat the more quickly it will gain weight, sleep becomes an intrusion, slowing down the process. So, in an exercise of absolute logic, the lights are kept on for more than 23 hours in every 24.

It would be nice to think that the odd half-hour of darkness is the product of some residual trace of compassion, allowing the creatures time for a quick nap. Unfortunately it isn't. Early broiler chicken growers tried keeping the lights on permanently, but sudden power cuts had a dramatic impact on the birds, causing panic and mass suffocation. This, of course, is not good for business and a token half-hour allows the birds to get used to the phenomenon of darkness just in case there should ever be a power cut.

But why were the lights so much brighter in the shed full of chicks? Again, logic holds the answer. The bright lights encourage the chicks to feed voraciously, but as they grow and the available space reduces, that energy can quickly turn into aggression. Fighting between birds can result in flesh damage or heart attacks. So the lights are dimmed.

Diet, of course, is the most fundamental way to manipulate any creature, including humans. Feed for broiler chickens consists of some 70 per cent cereals, the remainder being comprised of protein in the form of soya, meat, fish and bone and oils, vitamins and minerals. That simple, innocuous description doesn't, of course, tell the whole story. The 'meat' content can be the chickens themselves. There isn't a great demand for chicken heads, necks, blood, feathers, feet or offal in the high street and so it's not uncommon for these 'by products' to be recycled into low-grade chicken feed in a kind of cannibalistic merry-go-round.

Another immediately noticeable difference between the two sheds was the floor litter. Whereas in the first my feet kicked through light, dry, soft material, they now stood on something solid and with each step they stuck slightly. And the smell! For the six weeks of the broilers' almost non-stop eating spree the litter remains unchanged, coagulating with the accumulated droppings of 20,000 defecating chickens. The stench was completely pervasive and for months afterwards, whenever I smelt chicken cooking, that same smell pervaded the more obvious smell of roasting flesh.

In several places I noticed obviously dead chickens, mostly

on the margins of the shed, furthest from the food and water. Many others, again apart from the mainstream activity, sat motionless, eyes hooded, seeming almost to pant. Still others hobbled around on deformed feet, barely capable of movement.

I drew the attention of the guide to the dead and distressed creatures and instead of concern I received a lecture on efficiency and how the known percentage of mortalities are built into the stocking density. I was assured that someone would be coming through the shed shortly, as they did every day, to remove the dead chickens and cull those which were 'off their legs'.

Apparently, 3,000 of the 20,000 chickens in the shed would not survive the meagre six weeks allotted to them. Across the whole country, an estimated 72 million chickens (12 per cent of the national flock) die in this way every year.[1] It is a percentage which is inexorably increasing.

When you investigate what lies behind the innocuous expression 'off their legs', the findings are disturbing. The phenomenon begins at about day 35, approximately one week before slaughter, and the chickens remain squatting because it is too painful to stand up. They are killed because they are unable to reach either food or water and would eventually die of starvation and thirst. They are termed 'starve-outs'.

The cause is a direct result of the birds' rapid and unnatural growth rate. The chickens are faced with other stresses, but one of the main ones is their inability to form bones properly. What should be hard, calcified bone is frequently nothing more than soft cartilage. As a consequence, their skeletons fail to grow properly and their legs bend or break under their rapidly ballooning weight.

There is a silence surrounding this obvious welfare problem, caused partly by the shyness of producers and partly because university research programmes are increasingly the property of industrial clients and are not released publicly. One university study did look at this bone problem, but its findings were secret. However, some of the data was leaked to producers of BBC Television's *Horizon* programme, 'Fast Life in the Food Chain', transmitted in May 1992. The study found that of 1,000 broiler chickens from four different growers, 70 per cent had something wrong with the way they walked; 22 per cent were so badly affected they were presumed to be in chronic pain; and 5 per cent were virtually incapable of walking.

Even the Agricultural and Food Research Council, an industry quango which supports factory farming, stated at a press conference on chickens' leg deformities in March 1992 that up to four fifths of broiler chickens have broken bones and deformed feet and legs or other bone deformities.[2]

Professor John Webster, Head of the Department of Animal Husbandry at Bristol University and adviser to the Government on animal welfare, explained why:

> ...it is almost inevitable that in going for increased productivity and increased profitability, the incentive is to push animals right to their biological limits of capacity. By a combination of genetics and high quality food we have, in certain animals, particularly the broiler chicken, caused the animal seriously to outgrow its strength so that for the last 10 to 15 days of its short, 42-day life, there are severe abnormalities of bone development which we know to be painful and crippling.[3]

But even that isn't the end for the poor not-so-old broiler chicken! It seems incredible that a creature less than 42 days old could suffer from heart disease – but it does. It develops with the bird's increase in weight. With so much rapidly growing muscle tissue there is an increased demand for blood and the oxygen it carries. Unfortunately, the heart muscle isn't strong enough to cope and the cardio-vascular system comes under enormous stress. As a consequence, blood returning to the heart hits a kind of traffic jam and starts to build up in the veins. Plasma and fluids leak out and accumulate in the abdominal cavity in a process which is commonly known as 'dropsy' and more properly called 'ascites'.

The birds which I had seen sitting around the margins of the shed, panting and not eating, were almost certainly suffering from this. Of course, it is conceivable they were suffering from the third painful condition to affect broiler chickens...

The litter on which the birds were standing had increased five-fold in weight from the time it was first provided when they were day-old chicks. Their accumulated excreta simply builds up and the result is hock burns from the ammonia-laden litter. This ulcerated blistering affects not only their feet and legs but can also burn their breasts. No matter how badly affected, no matter how much pain they feel, the chickens can never escape the searing alkali which impregnates the floor on which they stand and walk and squat. It must be a constant, nagging, gnawing progressive burning and is completely ignored by growers. Any flesh which is damaged by the burning is simply discarded, the undamaged parts being sold as chicken pieces.

It's worth just briefly reconsidering the life of a broiler chicken. According to the Government's Farm Animal Welfare Council, intensive conditions have changed little over the past 30 years.[4] However, the birds' fast growth means that in the 1990s the vast majority of the 500–670 million killed annually in Britain[5] will endure their six-week existence with broken bones and deformities, heart disease and ammonia burns. It is a similar story in all other EC countries. In the USA, six billion broilers are killed each year,[6] of which 98 per cent are intensively reared in the same conditions as those described here.[7] We have turned a beautiful wild creature into this travesty of a living thing, something whose life is totally unsustainable without human intervention. Then we have the audacity to market the flesh as a health product and the intention, I'm afraid, is to make them grow even faster.

The industry's journal, *Poultry World*, states that 40 years ago, when the broiler industry started, it took a bird 84 days to reach the same weight which it now achieves in only 42 days.[8] Each year brings a reduction of one day in that growth time and in the USA, a 1.8 kg bird can be produced in 35 days.[9]

There are obvious and humanitarian ways to reduce the suffering of broiler chickens, the simplest being to reduce stocking densities, reduce the length of the artificially lit day and limit the food intake. But that, of course, is too immediate and too simple and doesn't involve sub-committees and research periods and consultative bodies *and no one makes money out of it.*

Dr Colin Whitehead of the Agricultural and Food Research Council, speaking on the *Horizon* programme, sums up the likely way forward:

I don't think it's right that we breed birds that are deformed but I think it's up to the skill of the geneticist and the breeder to try to solve these problems during the breeding process – in other words, to put selection pressure against these deformities so that the birds they produce would still be considered to be metabolically fit.[10]

However, it is precisely this system which has caused the

problem in the first place. Meanwhile, the suffering goes on.

Nowhere is it felt more acutely than in the turkey shed. But first I want to tell you a true story.

Some acquaintances went to a local farm in December 1994 to choose a turkey for Christmas. It was a family outing and they were expecting to survey an array of carcasses, neatly hanging, plucked and devoid of life. What they saw was a selection of very live birds, wandering around in all the bizarre gaudiness that turkeys are born with. Selection suddenly took on a very different dimension. From simple meat shoppers these people were transformed into dispensers of death.

The father tried to be very unemotional. 'Well, they're all going to die anyway!' But it was unconvincing.

Nevertheless, having settled on a turkey of the right weight, the decision was made. Then, as though by divine providence, the bird waddled up to them. At this, the younger daughter burst into tears and the elder daughter shouted out: 'How could you, Daddy?' and turned her back. When the farmer's hand reached out to grab Bert, because the bird had by now acquired a name, the whole family burst into tears.

The outcome was that Bert went home with them, but in the boot of the car, with all his feathers intact and very much alive. He is now the family pet and out of deference to him Christmas dinner that year was vegetarian. Now their whole diet is. Bert is an individual – a bit of a character with an enormous personality and a sense of both fun and mischief – and the whole family is horrified that they might have eaten him.

The whole point of this story is to counter the perception of farm animals as nothing more than programmed creatures with little individuality. They are, we are led to believe, almost entirely functional and imbued only with those abilities which are inherent in their genes – feeding, procreating, defecating – and incapable of learning or individual action. Anyone who has ever spent much time around animals knows this to be a total nonsense. However, the more we perceive animals to have a specific character or personality, the harder it is to close our eyes to their suffering. Which of us would allow our pet dog to lie in the corner whimpering in pain week after week? But those of us who eat meat allow something very similar to happen in our name.

Bert the turkey was lucky in that he was the product of a free range farm and was saved the hock and breast burns which most turkeys are forced to live with. But he too bears all the defects of human intervention that broiler chickens bear, again caused through selective breeding and dietary control.

Wild turkeys are striking and handsome and not even a fraction of the size of some of the white-feathered Christmas obscenities. The plumage of their wing and tail feathers is black, an iridescent black which shimmers with flashes of glistening red, green and copper hues, contrasting with their white wing bars. Like pheasants, they roost in trees but build their nests on the ground. They have an extraordinary defence mechanism – speed! When disturbed or threatened, they hurtle away in a whirring, rocketing explosion of flight, keeping low to the ground and hitting an incredible 88 km/h. They can keep this up for more than a kilometre and a half. Hardly surprising that such creatures have taken badly to intensive farming.[11]

The majority of the 38 million slaughtered annually in Britain spend their 12 to 26-week lives in conditions similar to broiler chickens or in pole barns, beginning at one day old when they are known as 'poults'.[12] Although pole barns do have natural light and ventilation, they are only a small improvement on broiler sheds and the turkeys are still subjected to appalling overcrowding and insanitary, leg-burning litter. Their natural diet of seeds, nuts, roots, grubs, grasses, legumes and the occasional slug or snail is substituted by a boring, endless regime of identical high-protein pellets.

The downfall of the turkey is its breast. The ability to afford a huge-breasted turkey for Christmas or Thanksgiving has become the touchstone of affluence for many. People sit around a groaning table, applauding a genetic monstrosity. The focal point of this festival of peace on Earth, or safe deliverance in the case of Americans, is a creature which has spent its life in abject misery, could barely walk and was a product of artificial insemination, because turkeys are no longer capable of natural procreation. The bloated breast, so lovingly carved, is the very thing which prevents the sexual organs of male and female turkeys from ever meeting. Not much of a celebration for them.

One would think that a festival based on all the more progressive aspects of the human psyche, proclaiming forgiveness, forbearance and goodwill, would involve a type of food which did not need to have its throat cut and which could barely walk.

One of the reasons why turkeys waddle, if they walk at all, is degeneration of the hip joints.[13] In this ball and socket mechanism, much of the weight is distributed through a pad of cartilage called the 'antitrochanter'. Under the stress of carrying a body that can reach 27 kg (the weight of an eight or nine-year-old child) in the largest breeding males, this structure breaks down, leading to degeneration of the joint. This is a result of the meat industry's constant drive to produce as much saleable meat as possible and as little of everything else – incidental things such as the skeleton – that has no retail value. And that means manipulating the shape of the animals to suit market demands.

Again, Dr Colin Whitehead of the Agricultural and Food Research Council has identified the scale of the problem.

Amongst the biggest and heaviest birds he put it as high as 70 per cent:

> When we look at the nature of these very severe lesions
> in turkeys it is probable that the birds are suffering pain
> rather than just discomfort.[14]

This conclusion is backed up by a worker at a Bernard Matthews farm who was secretly filmed for a Channel 4 documentary screened in December 1995 called 'This Turkey Business'. He explains that he has had to kill 400 birds in one day because 'they get various diseases because they're so intensive'. When asked why some birds were hobbling, he replied:

> They get leg problems here because the birds are so
> heavy the fluid in the knee joint...goes septic and then
> starts to go black, like blood poisoning all up the leg.
> They won't accept that down at the factory because that
> contaminates the whole line...we just kill it and throw it
> out and it goes for dog meat or for maggots for fishing.[15]

Many of the practices inflicted on battery hens and broiler chickens are also carried out on turkeys, including debeaking, and again, the problems of an inadequately developed heart lead to frequent heart attacks. Every year in Britain some two and a half million birds die from this and other diseases caused by intensive farming.[16] Growth-promoting antibiotics are routinely fed to both turkeys and broiler chickens.

Professor John Webster states in his book *Animal Welfare: A cool eye towards Eden*:

> Approximately one quarter of the heavy strains of
> broiler chicken and turkey are in chronic pain for

approximately one third of their lives. Given that poultry meat consumption in the UK exceeds one million tonnes per annum, this must constitute, in both magnitude and severity, the single most severe, systematic example of man's inhumanity to another sentient animal.[17]

The justification for all intensive rearing methods is always public demand – freedom of choice. The implication is that to restrict choice is somehow an affront on personal liberty. Yet we can't choose to run over old ladies on pedestrian crossings, drive without a safety belt or shout rude words at religious evangelists in the high street. Why should we have the choice to inflict suffering on sentient creatures? The freedom to choose is utterly valueless without freedom of information. I wonder how broiler chicken and turkey sales would be affected if they carried a Government health warning – perhaps something like: 'This bird was reared in pain in a rat-infested shed on disease-ridden bedding. It is endemically diseased. It is bad for your health, bad for the environment and is probably infected with salmonella which can kill you. Enjoy!'

As my introduction to the brave new world of intensive broiler chicken production came to an end and the shed door closed behind me, the tweeting of 20,000 birds, the stench of their living conditions and the sight of their pathos all disappeared. The sense of disgust, however, has always remained with me. I have the absolute conviction that we have produced a system which is unsustainable. Creatures which have little ability to live without human intervention, which need to be constantly medicated but are increasingly failing to survive, represent a disaster waiting to happen. And that's without even considering the morality of it.

4 ◆ THE END OF THE LINE

As I walked away from the shed I knew that later that evening the chicken catchers would go into action – local lads earning a bit on the side. In the near darkness they would grab handfuls of chickens by the legs – broken bones, hock burns and heart conditions notwithstanding – and cram them into cages for transport to the processing plant the following day. It was this plant that I now had to face. Again, what I saw then is typical of all modern processing plants in operation today.

The one I saw for the first time was not what I expected. It was an antiseptic model of efficiency in which time and motion studies had erased the waste of anything – even urinating time. When I spoke privately to one of the workers there, he told me about the company's 'bog book'. To avoid any possibility of time-wasting, all workers had to be logged into a book by their overseer every time they went to the lavatory. This way the company could keep trace of how often each person took a toilet break and how long it lasted. That gives a flavour of the management techniques which have helped turn chicken from a luxury into a food often cheaper in price than tomatoes.

As part of this model efficiency, a constant and predictable stream of birds has to be channelled down the lines and lorries arrive at preset times throughout the day, leaving a trail of white feathers behind them as they drive through the countryside.

As each lorry arrives, the birds are removed. In this particular plant it was done in a covered unloading bay adjoining the main building. Shackles dangled from a constantly moving, overhead conveyor system and the unloaders placed the feet of the chickens in the shackles so that the birds were slowly borne away, hanging head down, wings flapping feebly. It isn't difficult to imagine the effect on birds with broken bones or 27 kg turkeys with diseased hip joints.

The conveyor line of fluttering chickens disappeared through a hole in the wall, but before it did so it ran across the top of a large water-filled tank in such a way that the head and neck of each bird was immersed in it. The water was electrified, designed to stun. As the line continued past the tank, the flutterings stopped. In fact, apart from an occasional spasm, all movement ceased and the motionless, dripping animals disappeared from view.

I had initially undertaken not to witness the killing of the birds, but here was a whole industry based on slaughter and it seemed quite ludicrous that a 16-year-old should be so coy, so protected, that an event which now takes place more than 600 million times a year in one small country alone should somehow be too shocking to witness.

So I was taken into the main building and picked up the production line from where I had last seen it. The birds emerged still largely motionless and dripping from the electrified bath. The conveyor line took them past a man standing over a drain, clad from head to foot in white with a full-length waterproof apron.

His job consisted of two actions – with his left hand he took hold of a bird's head, then with the small sharp knife in his right hand he slashed the side of its neck. Blood immediately gushed out. He did it on and on and on, all day long. His hands and his apron, from chest to floor, were bright red with the blood of an endless line of miserable little creatures whose impoverished existence had been instigated by a multinational corporation and were now being clinically ended by it.

The workers in the plant, inured to this simple sight, hadn't woken up one day with a burning desire to work in a chicken killing and processing plant, but 'It's better than being on the dole!', as one of them put it to me. It seemed to me that in this little tableau was an encapsulation of our society's values. Eleven years of full-time education; public libraries and universities; centuries of great literature, music and painting; a struggle by political thinkers and philosophers to distil the essence of life – and this man was cutting throats because he had no other options.

The whole process of killing moved me in a way I least expected. I looked at the monotonous repetition, unemotional and matter-of-fact, which left a string of bloodied, gaping-necked creatures dangling as they moved forward in perpetual motion and I felt sorry for them. But no more sorry than I had felt for their miserable existence. What really affected me was the global brutality it represented.

The conveyor continued, dragging the birds through a bath of hot water known as the 'scalding tank'. Its purpose is to loosen the feathers. From here the carcasses went into the plucking machine where rubber fingers flailed the bodies, dragging the feathers out as they did so.

Design is a fascinating concept and it has enriched and improved our lives in innumerable ways. But if I were a designer, I wonder how I would react if someone rang me up and asked me to design something that would pull off a chicken's head. The answer, in fact, was quite simple – a kind of Archimedes screw which, with each revolution, pulled the head further from the body until eventually it simply tore it off.

Next stop was evisceration – disembowelling. Again, it was carried out automatically. A kind of metal spoon entered through the anal cavity and literally scooped out all that was inside. The same spoon was used for every chicken that passed by.

Washing, preparation and packing followed. Those chickens that were to be sold fresh were neatly wrapped, breast uppermost, in transparent plastic, each sitting on its own Styrofoam drip tray. Those to be frozen were delivered to the freezer department.

Within a few hours of entering the plant, each chicken was branded for the supermarket and adorned with glowing accolades – 'prime quality', 'premier grade', 'premium selection'. A bit like some geniuses, they had to wait for death before anything nice was said about them.

One brief inspection cannot reveal all, as I was later to find out. The immediate reaction of chickens when they are hung upside down is to raise their heads. This can mean that they completely miss the stunning bath and go to the blade fully conscious.

Even worse, technology moves on and the blood-spattered man with the knife has been replaced in many plants by an automatic cutter. Because not all chicken throats are identical, the position of the blade is not necessarily ideal. It can mean that some larger birds are cut on the breast and smaller ones on the head so that they both enter the scalding tank conscious.

Furthermore, even if the neck is cut, most automatic machines in current use sever the back or side of the neck and rarely cut the carotid arteries. This means that millions of birds are still conscious at this stage. A study involving three batches of broilers showed 6.8 per cent, 10 per cent and 23.4 per cent still not dead on entering the scalding tank.[1]

Dr Henry Carter, past President of the Royal College of

Veterinary Surgeons, states in the report:

> Procedures in far too many poultry slaughterhouses
> do not ensure that the birds are adequately stunned,
> leaving an unknown number alive and still conscious
> when they enter the scalding tank. It is high time that
> politicians and legislators put an end to practices
> that are unacceptable and inhumane.[2]

There are incidents throughout all our lives which are encapsulated and remembered with just one powerful visual image. The look from the boar was one such. As I left the processing plant I saw another. Huge lorries waited outside the loading bay and one of them was piled high with its empty wire cages. In the topmost tier was just one single crouching chicken, the blustering wind ruffling its feathers. I have no idea why it was there or what would eventually happen to it, but that solitary bird embodied my feelings on that day. It was then that I decided I would spend my life working to try and bring about change in a world where institutionalized cruelty seemed to pass without comment and where compassion was considered almost a crime.

5 ◆ SCIENCE, SADISM
   AND SALVATION

For the next few years of my life, between 16 and 21, I was largely occupied with my own education. It was the early 1980s and I was involved with campaigning on vegan and vegetarian issues at a local level. There was a gradual hardening of my views. Each new piece of information I sought out convinced me that giving up meat, fish and slaughterhouse by-products was not some fringe activity but central to the survival of the planet.

I was discovering, little by little, the role that meat plays in our culture, its inescapable link with the impoverishment of the developing world and its staggering influence on the major environmental problems which were gradually coming to light over this period. But what really motivated me was the extraordinary and widespread nature of cruelty to animals. I could not come to terms with the fact that it was almost impossible to order a meal that did not involve cruelty. But most of all, I could not understand the refusal of people to react even when they knew the truth. Such is the conviction of youth.

Does everyone think they're different from the norm? I suspect they do. In most respects I felt extremely normal and liked most of the things that teenage girls like – music, dancing, sex, having fun, doing stupid things and having friends. But there were areas where I was very much on my own, where I could look to no one for support and where invariably I felt isolated. It was usually because I couldn't keep my mouth shut about cruelty to animals.

I had already organized high street petitions against all kinds of abuse in various parts of the globe but when I went to sixth-form college in Stockport, Cheshire, I was actually confronted with it. The first occasion was on studying for biology A level when, for practical lessons, students were drawn from other groups and class sizes could reach 60 or more.

For my first dissection lesson, I arrived in the classroom to find a newly killed rat on the cutting board – one for every student. They were still warm and rigor mortis had not yet set in. It is highly unlikely that cutting up an animal would ever have any part to play in the working lives of even one of the students present in that laboratory. It is also highly questionable whether they would learn anything they could not discover from numerous other teaching aids that would not have involved death. And a similar scene is repeated in sixth forms and colleges across the world.

The ageing, balding lecturer with tired eyes gave out matter-of-fact instructions as to how to prepare the rat for dissection. We were supposed to place it on its back, stretch out its limbs as if for crucifixion and pin it through its paws to the board beneath.

I looked at the rat in front of me and was disgusted by this casual violence. This institutionalized belittling of life was, I felt, part of the problem which faced society, not part of its cure. The rat is highly intelligent, some say more intelligent than a dog, and has developed complex social patterns (which is why vivi-sectionists frequently use it for behavioral studies – although what relevance that has to human behaviour I fail to see). And what have we done with this rodent, a species whose time on the globe far outstrips ours? We call it vermin and allow anyone to do anything they like to it. In this case 60 were needlessly killed for an A level practical.

I wanted no part of it, stood up and told the lecturer so. There was no obvious reaction in his eyes, but he offered no objection and I sensed an unspoken understanding of my views.

As I left the lecture room I caught sight of the rest of the class, mostly eyes averted, concentrating intently on the simple job in front of them for fear that by looking at me they would be identified with my views. That is a reaction I have grown used to over the years. Despite this and other refusals to take part in dissection, I passed my biology A level.

I went on to Reading University to read pure zoology, but was horrified by more needless dissection. The first two terms were the most difficult as they involved endless dissection and had to be completed before it was possible to elect specific components. To begin with, I attended the lectures, remained silent, watched what other people did but took no direct part. I illustrated my work by copying the drawings from textbooks.

On one occasion, a tray of newly killed blackbirds was brought into the laboratory and distributed amongst the students. So cavalier was the approach that there were many more birds than students. Life was considered so cheap, of such little importance, that they could not even bother to count the number needed.

As time went by I became more vociferous about my beliefs in front of the other students and eventually the lecturers as well. The strange thing was that my objections were noted but no one attempted to justify the dissections as a vital part of the degree process. In the end I passed the first-year practical exams with a B.

Perhaps it was *naïveté*, but I really did not have a clear idea

of what would be involved in my chosen degree. The component I intended to take was embryology, but at the first lecture
part of the shell of a chicken's egg was removed, exposing the
little chick and its beating heart. It seemed to me that we were
being asked to desecrate life before it had even started. I
walked out.

After that I tried entomology, but having just watched the
extraordinarily powerful *Animal's Film* by Victor Schonfeld, I
was in no mood for compromise. This was the film chosen to
launch Channel 4 TV in Britain and is almost two hours of
heart-rending revelation of the way we treat animals – from
food to fur. It has become almost the definitive film on animal
abuse.

The first act I was expected to do on the entomology course
was place a pin in either end of a maggot and pull in opposite
directions, tearing it apart. This time I spoke out forcibly to the
tutor and was eventually called to see my head of department,
who accused me of being too vocal.

Next it was parasitology, but that involved cutting up
animals infected with parasites, so I moved on to invertebrates.
This was the most shocking of my experiences. A pan full of
crabs had been boiled while alive in order to kill them before
dissection. I touched one and despite all that it had been
through, it moved. It was still alive. On this occasion when I
expressed my anger I was backed up by other students. The
lecturer was visibly shaken and she walked out of the class.

I decided it was impossible for me to continue with pure
zoology, although that is what I had always wanted to study, so I
opted for a joint degree – zoology and psychology. In fact it was
to prove the most useful degree I could have done. I studied the
communication of dolphins, whales and also chimpanzees, and
my practical project was on ethology – the study of animals in
the wild. I chose feral cats.

Part of the degree was the study of farm animals and I chose to look at the effect factory farming has on an animal's natural behaviour. It is one thing to state this in intuitive, even emotional terms and that's something I'm always being accused of. But to observe it carefully, measure it, quantify it and then set it out as a proposition in scientific terms which can be justified and defended is something else. I face so much rhetoric and blatant lying about the way animals are kept that I am grateful to have been able to prove that the way in which we rear them destroys their natural behaviour and therefore virtually destroys them.

On leaving university I was desperate to work in animal rights but was forced to spend the first few months teleselling advertising space for *Media Week* in London. This was not part of the grand design! But after six months I got what I wanted and I still have the champagne bottle (empty now, of course) which fuelled the celebration.

I became a research officer with an anti-vivisection organization in the summer of 1986. Now I was into animal rights at the deep end and even my previous research had not prepared me for the abysmal and sickening nature of some of the things I had to deal with. Many of the tortures which passed for experiments were recorded on video by the teams responsible and I had the misfortune to witness dozens of them.

This book is not about vivisection but about my motivation, my beliefs and imperatives. Some of these were formed during this period and are therefore relevant. What I witnessed there made me ashamed of many scientists and disgusted me to a degree that I still find hard to cope with.

I have no intention of listing a string of abuses carried out on living creatures by people without a single shred of pity or compassion, but I will tell two brief stories. Both came to light as a result of the videos made of them, the first shot by vivisectors themselves, and publicised by animal rights organizations such as People for the Ethical Treatment of Animals (PETA) in the USA. They are both unforgivable and say much more about the natures of those who carried out the tortures than they do about so-called scientific investigation.

The first 'experiment' was performed at the University of Pennsylvania head injury department, in Philadelphia, in 1984 and involved a big baboon.[1] He was strapped to a table fully conscious and his head immobilized in a helmet. His head was then subjected to a huge impact – which was not powerful enough to kill him but strong enough to cause obvious excruciating pain and brain damage.

The baboon was then released from his restraints and as his head lolled about, hopelessly out of control, a woman vivisector can be heard saying, 'There he goes!' She then adds, 'You'd better hope the anti-vivisectionists don't get hold of this video.' Still holding the injured animal, the group burst into laughter.

The excuse offered for this unspeakable assault was that it would assist car design and help avoid injury. I don't want to go into the irrelevance of animal experiments or the morality of commerce inflicting such pain for profit, but the record of some motor manufacturers is that of cynical disregard rather than an altruistic search for improvements. At that time, when dangers were identified, the first thing the manufacturers did was equate the cost of likely law suits with the cost of making changes to the design. Whichever was the cheaper tended to dictate what action they took. The baboon's suffering was almost certainly part of this cynicism.

The second case concerned Britches, a newborn stumptail macaque monkey. Ungainly, with large sticky-out ears, he was nevertheless beautiful. Like any other baby macaque, he would have had huge round eyes and would have spent the early months, even years of his life clinging to his mother. Neither of those things applied to Britches because immediately after birth at the University of California's research centre at Riverside, Los Angeles, in 1985, he was removed from his mother and his eyelids were stitched together.[2]

The stitches which blinded him were not even the neat, surgical sutures of experience but huge crude stitches with thick twine, the stitches of indifference, the equivalent of stitching a human's eyes with string.

So desperate was this little creature for comfort that he would cling on to and hug anything placed in his cage – a blanket, a small cuddly toy, anything. But, deprived of all comfort, all maternal care, and kept in a sterile and barren cage without stimulation, he was mostly allowed only a padded cylinder to cling to.

Watching one animal inflict such intense suffering on another, particularly one so innocent and uncomprehending is, undoubtedly, the worst sight I have ever seen in my life. And the reason for this experiment? To determine the effect of blindness on children. The vivisectors at the University of California excused their use of the monkey by saying that the daily routine of children's lives made it too difficult to work with them.

What type of mind could have conceived of this and, perhaps more importantly, could have carried it out?

The wide-ranging work I did on vivisection led me to conclude that most vivisectors fall into one of two categories. To the first, all that matters is cause and effect. They have absolutely no concept of suffering and no conscience about what they do. They storm into the laboratory, administer the injections or shocks or force feeding, storm out again and await the results. They are, in its truest interpretation, the psychopaths of science.

The second type is the sadist. We have been brought up

with a belief, repeated and reinforced every time a vivisector talks about their work, that they partake in it unwillingly and in our best interests. It's nonsense. Many of these people obviously get a buzz out of the torture they administer and the name of the game is power. There is not a shadow of doubt in my mind that they would do these same things to humans without a second thought if it were given legitimacy. There was no shortage of scientists and doctors eager to carry out unspeakable experiments on humans at Buchenwald and other concentration camps. Perhaps even more frightening, there were almost no lengths to which British and US security forces would not go in order to spirit these people out of Germany at the end of the war and save them from trial in order to have access to their knowledge. This sadistic breed of scientists did not suddenly appear from nowhere and live only in Nazi Germany. They exist everywhere.

The story of Britches has a happier ending than most vivisection victims. He was released from his misery when still a young baby, the stitches removed from his eyes and the long and painful process of trying to repair the acute psychological damage undertaken. It would be nice to think that this compassionate response was initiated by the vivisectors responsible for his pain – but it wasn't. It was made possible only because the Animal Liberation Front (ALF) broke into the laboratories and released him, finding a loving and caring refuge where he would be safe.

It's quite difficult for me when asked by journalists about my views on the ALF. The question is usually posed in conjunction with alleged ALF violence against humans and I know that any vaguely supportive response will be used as a stick with which to beat me and my organization, particularly as I work so much with young people. Of course I don't support any action that endangers human life or safety. But when I look at footage of Britches' abysmal life at the hands of his vivisectors and then a few months after his rescue, my heart goes out to those who were brave enough to risk their own liberty to release him from such a squalid existence.

Despite the appalling nature of the things I had to deal with, I at last believed I was helping animals. But my first lesson in internal politicking was about to be learned. It erupted in such a devastating way that it almost destroyed the organization.

But I found a new job to go to and it offered exciting prospects – youth education officer with the Vegetarian Society. I was faced with the challenge of starting a whole department from scratch. Up to this point the organization had done no campaigning work, largely building its reputation as a food and information organization over a period of 150 years. Now, in 1987, I was starting with a clean slate and a brief to concentrate on young people – those who hold the key to a more compassionate tomorrow. I decided my long-term goal was to try and bring about a change in national attitudes. Such determination is easy when you're 23.

The following seven years of constant campaigning gave me the skills and the experience eventually to found a new and dynamic charity – Viva! (Vegetarians International Voice for Animals).

6 ◆ MILKY BAR KIDOLOGY

One of the most rewarding aspects of my work at the Vegetarian Society and now at Viva! has been the school talks I initiated. The talks were also the stick with which the National Farmers' Union (NFU) (not a union at all but the employers' body) and the Meat and Livestock Commission (MLC) thought it possible to beat me. (The MLC was set up by the Government in 1967, with Government money, and is still monitored by it. Its remit is to promote red meat sales and its income derives from a levy on every slaughtered carcass with some funding still coming from the Government.) But no matter how much these bodies huffed and puffed about indoctrinating 'children', conveniently ignoring the age range of mainly between 14 and 18, it had little or no impact. They gave the impression that, somehow, we forced our way into schools – presumably disguised as dinner ladies – and held classes forcibly in their seats with Kalashnikovs while we perverted their minds. What really worried them, of course, and still does, is the effect that discovery has on young people. It is astounding that they can grow to virtual adulthood and know almost nothing of how animals are reared and killed. That cannot be accidental.

When young people do find out about or actually them-selves witness cruelty to animals, they tend not to turn the other cheek. To them, as mentioned earlier, cruelty is cruelty and they are not ashamed to show their feelings, their disgust and desire to stop it. Many adults appear to be frightened by emotion. Anything which challenges, disturbs or upsets them is pushed into the darker recesses of the mind and they pretend there is nothing that can be done about it. Part of the reason is that if they accept something is wrong and should be changed, it automatically requires something of them, some action, some change in their lifestyle. And that is simply too demanding. Young people, on the other hand, believe they have the power to change the world.

The two things which motivate them most of all are cruelty to animals and the destruction of the environment. I say this after having given hundreds of talks in hundreds of schools and colleges to perhaps tens of thousands of young people. Insultingly, their concerns are so often dismissed as a fad or fashion by adults with barely a shred of their knowledge. When they make the decision to become vegetarian they are frequently put under huge pressure by their parents and friends and yet many of them sustain their beliefs – hardly the stuff that fads are made of.

I remember one 15-year-old who came to me in tears. She had listened to me talk and had watched the video footage of factory farming. She knew it to be true – her father was a pig farmer operating an intensive system. He had refused to allow her to become vegetarian, saying he would have no such thing in his house. This kind of situation is always a dilemma and any advice or support that I offered might be interpreted as pitting child against parent.

But I honestly believe that if you start to retreat from conflict there is no point in going on. In fact, it was precisely this type of dilemma that led me to launch the 'Convert-a-Parent' campaign as Viva!'s opening shot when the charity was launched in October 1994. It provided all the information necessary for young people to reassure their parents that by giving up meat they wouldn't turn into shrivelled little weeds or die from malnutrition.

In the case of the pig farmer's daughter, I provided her with what information and encouragement I could, suggesting tactful ways in which she might like to handle the situation. Some months later I received a letter from her saying that she was now vegetarian and, what's more, her father frequently ate the same meals as her. The determination and courage it takes to see something like that through to the end has my total admiration.

So often parents claim their opposition stems from concern for their children, but unfortunately it is often more about control or inconvenience. Nevertheless, things are improving and these days the most frequent requests from parents are for nutritional information and the letters of abuse have become rare. That marks a huge step forward.

But still, with our few thousand pounds' expenditure, we are accused of indoctrination. No mention is ever made of the multimillion-pound marketing spend targeted on schools by the NFU, MLC and companies such as McDonalds. It includes trips around special free-range farms, videos, the magazine *Meat Messenger*, course materials and even hamburger vouchers as school prizes. No mention of factory farming is ever made. This is what I would call indoctrination because the message is essentially untrue. It's prime mover is the MLC through its British Meat Education Service. And it starts young – with primary school children.

Shortly after the launch of Viva! I did something which I have never done before and conducted a three-way school talk with the NFU and a butcher. Each of us put our case and at the end those in the class who agreed with vegetarianism were asked to put their hands up. About 90 per cent did so. The input of the farmers' lobby made no difference whatsoever.

I conduct school talks in a standard way. I am normally invited as part of food technology or sometimes PSE (personal and social education) classes. For the first 20 minutes I show a video. I then talk for a similar length of time and take questions.

Over the years I think I have heard almost every possible question connected with vegetarianism and the main ones are predictable: 'What will happen to all the animals?' 'How do you know vegetables don't feel pain?' 'We're meant to eat meat, aren't we?' 'Where will I get my protein?' Some of them are endearing when they come from kids, but when the same questions are put accusingly by a 50-year-old MLC spokesman, it verges on the pathetic.

One of the most enlightened and questioning schools I have ever spoken at was run by an order of nuns. At the end of the talk I asked if anyone intended becoming vegetarian and 45 out of 50 put their hands up. At the back of the class sat an extremely old and wrinkled little nun who had listened intently throughout the hour's talk, her eyes barely ever leaving me. I had constantly been expecting some kind of intervention from her but it hadn't happened. As I looked at the forest of young arms held high in the air I was amazed to see this parched and wrinkled, almost transparent little arm suddenly begin to rise, hesitantly at first but then shooting aloft with total conviction. I was delighted.

Every survey in recent years has consistently shown that the proportion of young people who are vegetarian is considerably higher than the adult population. I hope I have played a part in their education.

The bulk of my energies has gone into explaining the vegetarian imperatives. It is important to provide people with attainable goals. Very few people turn from being meat eaters into vegans, bypassing vegetarianism. The culture shock is usually too great.

It is important that any step a person takes should be encouraged. If the first move is to give up battery eggs, that is a step forward; no longer eating red meat, that is a positive move; cutting out factory-farmed animals is also an important decision. I do believe passionately and with total conviction that veganism has to be the ultimate goal, but I am convinced that all steps along that route are valid and help to save the suffering of animals.

Having said that, the cruelty of the dairy industry has traditionally been ignored by some vegetarian interests and I feel it cannot remain so any longer. The final trigger for my becoming vegan was sudden and very close to home – in fact, in the field which adjoins my house, on a summer's day in 1994.

I had just been reading a report by the national tourist board which had carried out a survey amongst American tourists to find out their likes and dislikes of Britain. Topping their list of disappointments was the lack of cows in our fields. The survey was conducted in the early spring, before most of the cattle had been released from the imprisonment of their winter sheds. The tourists had arrived expecting to see the agricultural chequerboard of our countryside dotted with grazing black-and-white Friesian dairy cows. Had they been here in summer, though, they would have barely been able to swing a camcorder for the density of cattle, particularly in Cheshire, where I live, a county which is virtually one huge intensive dairy farm.

Four pregnant heifers arrived in the field alongside my garden in mid-May. Heavy with calf, they spent the early summer in idyllic surroundings – a lush meadow bordered by a wood and a meandering river. When one of them unexpectedly gave birth to a perfect little bull calf amidst the long grass one sunny evening, the idyll was complete. I stood and watched as the mother lovingly licked her offspring from head to foot, unhurriedly, calmly and with transparent contentment. Eventually she rose to her feet and gently nudged the little calf to his feet with her muzzle. Age-old instincts were prompting her to ensure that he was capable of flight if the need arose.

The next day, the farmer and the cowhand arrived in the field and the idyll was over. The cowhand carefully scooped the calf into his arms and walked away with him, the heifer following behind without any need of ropes or tethers, concerned for the welfare of her young. They disappeared up the lane towards the farmyard.

After another day of suckling on the colostrum, which precedes the milk flow and ensures the calf's ability to resist disease, he and his mother were separated as they always are – she to begin her twice-daily sessions in the milking parlour, he to face life in a barren shed.

This particular cow, No. 324, was unusual in that this was her eighth calf, making her probably 10 years old. It was, I was told, her last and after she had finished this lactation she would be slaughtered. Perhaps you could consider her lucky – lucky to have borne eight calves and had each one removed from her at a day or two old – because most dairy cows produce no more than two or three calves and are killed at about five years old.[1] Left to their own devices they would live for 20 years or more.

The whole business of the pregnancy is about producing milk and in many ways the calves are simply a by-product. The females are largely kept to replenish the dairy herd while most of the male calves are simply not wanted – too scrawny for beef, the wrong sex for milk, they are good for nothing but veal. There is something particularly disgusting about a business which is based on such undeniable greed.

According to Dr Peter Jackson, Head of the Farm Animals Division, Cambridge Veterinary School, the poor old cow produces 10 times more milk than her calf could ever drink[2] but such are the marketing imperatives that all of it must be extracted for human use, even though it may never be consumed because of the overproduction. Are we so lacking in compassion that we must deny even suckling, the most basic of instincts, to a creature which has paid an extremely dear price for its docility?

It is dietary control and genetic manipulation which has led to this enormous output of milk – the average of a 'good cow' is 25 to 30 litres a day,[3] three times the volume cows were producing only 50 years ago. A high yielding cow now produces a staggering 45 litres (80 pints) of milk a day.[4] It carries with it a cost, all borne by the cow. She has a one in three chance of her udders secreting pus and painfully swelling with mastitis.[5] The obviously painful process of forcing antibiotics up her teats is unsuccessful in controlling the disease.

It is the same story in the USA, where the number of cows raised for milk dropped from almost 22 million in 1950 to 10.8 million in 1980, yet the amount of milk rose from 116 billion pounds to 128 billion.[6] Each cow is producing so much milk that she is being pushed beyond her biological limits.

If you look at any herd in Europe or the USA going in for milking you will see the huge and unnatural shape of the cows' udders, a distortion of what they should be. Because of the strain of carrying the ludicrously over-sized udders and the fact that they distort the natural conformation of her legs, there is also a one in three chance that the cow will develop painful diseases of the feet.[7] Professor John Webster, Head of the Department of Animal Husbandry at Bristol University, states that inspection of the feet of cull cows at slaughter reveals evidence of past or present foot damage in almost 100 per cent of animals.[8] Damage often results in laminitis, a disease which the Ministry of Agriculture says causes 'great pain to the cow'.[9] Tissue lining the foot becomes inflamed and may lead to ulcers. Professor Webster explains, 'To understand the pain of laminitis it helps to imagine crushing all your fingernails in the door then standing on your fingertips.'[10] Almost every cow, at some point in her life, is living with this painful and crippling disease. Foot diseases are difficult to cure and are frequently left untreated.

When a combination of feet and udders becomes so great it starts to affect the cow's milk yield, she will be sent to slaughter and used for burgers, school meals, baby foods and other 'low-quality' products.

It isn't only mastitis and hock problems which send the dairy cow to the slaughterhouse. Some go because they are simply worn out and no longer sufficiently productive for the balance sheet. They can 'lose body tissue', a polite way of saying they become emaciated. The evidence is there in almost every dairy herd. If you look beyond the scene of apparent tranquillity, particularly at the hind quarters of grazing animals, you will often see little more than a skin-covered coat rack. In advanced cases the eyes sink into the head and the coat becomes rough, owing to the lack of moisture under the skin. This can be associated with a complete breakdown of the tissues of the udder.

In fact the dairy cow, which appears to have a better deal than most farm animals, is a remarkable model of deception. She is worked beyond her capacity to cope, which is why, since the Second World War, the average number of lactations has reduced from eight to four[11] and why UK dairy farmer F. Wesley Abbey states in his report on the feeding and breeding of dairy cows that in the USA commercial dairy farmers are only interested in producing more milk:

Legs, feet, stature and even quality come a long way
down their list of importance. With a culling rate of 35
to 40 per cent per year, there is little interest in a cow
that will last.[12]

Only three months after giving birth and while still milking
heavily, she will be reimpregnated, usually by artificial insemination. Only for the last few weeks of her pregnancy will she go
dry. For nine months of every year she carries the double bur-
den of milking and pregnancy, her udders working 10 times
harder than they would under natural conditions.

Now, you would think that in return for this constant and
uncomplaining production-line lifestyle, the dairy cow would
earn our thanks. Not a bit of it. Dr David Beever, Head of Ruminant Nutrition and Metabolism at the Agricultural and Food
Research Council, speaking on the BBC *Horizon* programme
'Fast Life in the Food Chain', is not finished with them yet:

> We can look at the efficiency with which a cow is
> converting forages into milk energy by looking at the
> overall energetics – of the 72,000 calories a cow con-
> sumes every day, 19,000 are converted into milk – and
> she is not very efficient… I see little evidence that we
> are working these cows too hard and if we care to look
> across into Europe, and particularly look into the
> United States, then we have got cows that are working
> a lot harder through both genetic improvement and
> nutritional improvements. So I would certainly not
> agree that we have got these cows to their limits.[13]

Fortunately, there is a countervailing view and in this instance it
comes from Professor John Webster, speaking on the same
programme:

The dairy cow is a supreme example of an overworked mother. She is by some measures the hardest worked of all our farm animals and it can be scientifically calculated. It is equivalent to a jogger who goes out for six to eight hours every day, which is a fairly lunatic pursuit. In fact the only humans who work harder than the dairy cow are the cyclists in the Tour de France, which is the ultimate in masochism really.[14]

And even they only do it for a couple of weeks or so.

As though that was not enough, the Government has allowed experimentation in 15 herds with a drug called bovine somatotropin (BST) which increases a cow's milk yield by 40 per cent[15] and mastitis by up to 45 per cent.[16] It is a growth hormone which essentially stimulates the cow into diverting more of its nutrients into making milk and is injected directly into the animal on a daily basis. The farms involved in these trials have been kept secret and the milk produced by the cows has been included in the public milk supply without any real tests on its safety for humans or cows. The testing sites have only become public knowledge because of detective work and enquiries by organizations such as the Food Commission, which showed that areas supplying London's milk were included in the trials.[17]

The general use of BST has been banned in the EC and its future use depends upon decisions made by the EC on 1 January 2000. However, MAFF state in a report, *Bovine Somatotropin Update*, that limited field trials in the UK are continuing.[18]

In the USA in 1995 about 15 per cent of dairy cows were routinely injected with bovine growth hormone[19] (BST is a genetically engineered version of BGM), which increased milk production by up to 20 per cent, causing cows' udders to become so heavy and swollen that some dragged along the ground. The cows' stepping on their udders caused them to become infected and increased mastitis.[20]

Jim Barnard, British milk producer and Liberal Democrat politician, stated in *Farming News* in June 1995 that Britain imports products from BGH milk, adding:

> Either the drug is considered unsafe and foreign dairy products using it should not be on sale, or our farmers should be able to use it. The Government can't have it both ways.[21]

In 1994, when the UK imported 4,000 tonnes of mozzarella cheese from the US, a third of the farmers were using BGH.

But who needs BST when the latest experiments, again in Cheshire, involve breeding from European cows who can produce double the current output of milk without it?

As for the offspring of these and all other dairy cows, I will come to them later *(see p.83 and pp.91–100).*

7 ◆ A TALE OF THE SEA

Campaigning was at the heart of my new youth strategy when I began work at the Vegetarian Society and it was paying off. Junior membership rose from less than 200 to 6,000 in the three years from 1987 to 1990. I had a committed and enthusiastic team and we were influencing tens of thousands of young people, helping them to become vegetarian, helping to save animals.

To begin with, in the days before word processors, we tried to reply to every letter by hand on the day it was received, because it kills the enthusiasm of young people to wait weeks for a standard, typed reply. When it got that I was still in the office at 10 p.m. or later, writing away, and the post was bring-ing 900 new letters every day, it was obvious the team would have to grow. It did and I became Youth Education Manager.

We were conducting school talks with a purpose-made video, *Food without Fear*, which was a winner at the New York Film and TV Festival. As a result of a campaign called 'SCREAM!!', which showed the reality of factory farming, interest in vegetari-anism amongst young people blossomed and the number of school projects on the subject increased 10-fold.

Despite this, school caterers were not responding and were still largely offering meat and two veg. as school lunch. That led me to launch the campaign called 'CHOICE!' aimed at increasing the number of schools offering a vegetarian alternative for lunch. It was a huge success, increasing the numbers from around 13 per cent of all secondary schools to 65 per cent. We all felt delighted that we were now influencing the nation as a whole.

As the membership grew so did the need for our own magazine and there was a real sense of achievement when *Greenscene* was launched, a 40-page magazine for young people. Eventually, when it was necessary to pass this on to someone else in the department to run, it was a sad day for me.

At the same time I was expanding my knowledge of the issues and this tempered any temptation there might have been to become complacent. Whatever success we were having it seemed as little compared with the overall world-wide trends and the universal mass slaughter of animals. As the 1980s progressed, developing countries began to adopt the West's appalling intensification methods and were encouraged to model themselves on us. Environmental destruction accelerated and I could feel, ever more firmly, the reverberations of human footprints, metaphorically stamping across the creatures and habitats of the world. A little was getting better, but an awful lot was getting worse.

Along with many concerned environmental scientists, I felt the globe was approaching a watershed when it would be too late to reverse the devastation and misery which humankind was increasingly spreading. It was as though our touch was poisoned by some virus and everywhere we went, everything we handled, we left in a worse condition than when we found it. Governments took research and found ways of belittling it; they were given information and warnings and ignored them; they had the knowledge and resources to change people's destructive habits but used those resources to increase the destruction.

That's how it was then, that's how I felt then and nothing has changed.

The rape of our oceans typifies the relentless progress towards greater destruction of creatures and ecosystems. We have the knowledge to predict the outcome of this onslaught and yet we do nothing to prevent it.

In March 1994, the United Nations Food and Agriculture Organization (UNFAO) published a paper, *State of the World: Fisheries and Aquaculture*, which should have sent a shudder running around the world.[1] It stated that of the world's 17 main fishing grounds, nine were facing potentially catastrophic declines in some species, while the remaining areas were already being exploited to the limits of their capacity. When a sober and restrained organization like UNFAO uses the word 'catastrophe', it probably means that the four horsemen of the apocalypse have already been seen taking tea at the Ritz. However, instead of outrage, the reaction was jingoistic nationalism and the ensuing debate was not about corrective measures but about rights and quotas.

The main cause of the crisis is overfishing, but the stocks are under pressure for other reasons, not least industrial and agricultural pollution, tourist and fish farm developments and the gradual poisoning of the entire marine ecosystem by highly toxic chemicals, with heavy metals and polychlorinated biphenyls (PCBs) at the top of the list.

To understand the scale and speed of the destruction it's important to look at the rate of decline in fish stocks. In 1950, the known catches of fish around the world amounted to 22 million tons. By 1989 they had risen to 100 million tons. For the following three years they dropped to a maximum figure of 97 million tons despite huge investment in new ships, expensive satellite navigation systems and fish finders and the purchasing of rights to exploit the coastal waters of developing countries.[2] Inherent in this decline is a warning which seems to go unheeded – the seas cannot sustain the onslaught for much longer.

There have been numerous previous warnings but international fishing is uncontrollable and amounts to little more than anarchy. When restraint has worked for one species it has been at the expense of others. Once, along the north-east coast of Britain, there were seemingly endless shoals of herring. By the 1950s the first signs of decline were obvious, but uncontrolled fishing continued. In 1978 a halt was called, by which time the shoals had been virtually destroyed. Only now are east-coast herring making something of a comeback. But such powers of recovery can't be relied upon.

The 1970s cod war, in which Iceland unilaterally extended its fishing grounds by imposing a 200-mile (322-km) limit around its shores, was a sign of things to come. It was brought about by the profligacy of the British fleets, largely from Grimsby, Hull and Fleetwood, at that time the largest fishing ports in the world. Fish was a cheap, plentiful and little-valued commodity and much of it wasn't even eaten but finished up in fertilizer factories.

The fish fertilizer factories are still in existence, along with dozens of other 'industrial' users of fish for products such as catering oils, feed for farmed fish and other animals, and even oil for candles, and as much as 50 per cent of all fish caught in the northern hemisphere may end up not on someone's plate but in the polish they use to shine their shoes.[3] Some species, such as sand eels and ling, are caught in their millions of tonnes for just these purposes.

The Icelandic action to exclude British trawlers was presented as an action to preserve fish stocks and placed them on the moral high ground. It was a deceit. In 1985 Icelandic trawlers took 400,000 tonnes of cod from their waters, but even without the predations of the British fleet, stocks continued to shrink. By 1993 the allowed catches were reduced by almost a half to 220,000 tonnes. Still stocks declined. For 1995, allowed catches have been cut to 163,000 tonnes in the fading hope that numbers will recover.[4]

Part of the problem is the method of fishing used to catch cod – trawling. Nets like a huge sock are used and the mouth of the sock can be 70 metres wide. The top is kept open with buoyancy devices and along the bottom are tickler chains, designed to drive fish from their hiding places on the bottom and up into the mouth. To keep the net open, huge, metal-bound, wooden 'otter' boards are fixed on either side of the opening at an angle so that as they are dragged through the water they naturally pull the mouth of the net open. They can weigh tonnes and crush and grind to destruction anything in their path. They effectively plough the sea-bed to a depth of several centimetres, destroying all life in their path. And they do it day after day in their thousands, to and fro across the same fishing grounds.[5]

The most recently publicised battles for fish have been between Spain and Canada off Newfoundland, and between Spain and Britain's Cornish fishermen off the Bay of Biscay. The Canadian experience is even more frightening than Iceland's and again involves cod. In 1990, catches totalled 400,000 tonnes and yet a year later they were down by almost a half.[6] In 1992, they amounted to just 70,000 tonnes and in the following year, they were just a few thousand tonnes.[7] The environmental costs are incalculable and will affect a myriad of other creatures who form part of what was once a finely-balanced ecosystem.

All across the world, countries are at each other's throats over the right to exploit particular stretches of water. A dispute over resources is the classic ingredient of warfare and we are seeing this develop around the globe.

In the summer of 1994 I sailed on a trawler to see the fishing process – not a deep-sea vessel but one of the smaller, English south-coast fishing fleet. The method is identical, it is just the scale which is different. Once the otter boards and nets have been 'shot' (lowered), all that serves as a reminder of what's happening on the sea-bed are the taut wire hawsers which drag the net behind the slowly moving vessel. The stench of diesel fuel and putrefied fish slime is a constant accompaniment.

Once fish enter the net, they are funnelled down it into a narrow sleeve known as the 'cod end'. The first fish in are dragged along for hours and may 'drown' because in the crush, as other fish pile on top of them, their gills are unable to extract oxygen from the water. Then, as they are hauled up through hundreds of metres of water, the difference in pressure can cause their eyes to balloon out or their swim bladders to burst.

A common grouse amongst the deckhands and the skipper was 'fish quotas'. These were introduced under the EC's Common Fisheries Policy (CFP) on advice from the International Council for the Exploration of the Sea (ICES) and are known as Total Allowable Catches (TACs). Under this scheme, fisher-men are told how many of each species they may catch, but once they have reached their limit for one type of fish they are allowed to carry on fishing for other types. Often different species swim together, such as cod and haddock, so even though the quota for haddock has been reached they are still caught together with the cod.[8] There have been numerous press and TV reports of trawlers with secret holds in which these illegal catches are hidden, but the more usual course is to return them to the sea. None of them survive. The official EC figure for discarded haddock is over 40 per cent of all those caught, but other, independent estimates, put the figure at 60 per cent.[9]

Those that are still alive when they are thrown back present a particularly sad spectacle. They form a silver trail astern of the boat, thrashing their tails spasmodically as they try to dive below the waves, only to float back up again. Gulls swarm above them, snatching an easy meal. Some research puts the global proportion of caught fish returned to the sea as high as 30 per cent.[10] Also shovelled back with the debris from the net is a selection of every crawling, creeping and swimming creature which goes to make up the complex environment of the sea-bed. They, too, are dead or dying.

The introduction of fish quotas had little to do with conservation in the first place, but was rather an attempt to ration out the spoils in order to avoid conflict. It seems to have, if anything, made matters worse all round.

Fish don't feel pain! Who could ever have conceived of such a lame excuse to justify a total absence of controls over how fish live and die? And who would have believed that so many people could be taken in by it? Fish have a complex central nervous system and part of its function is to send messages of pain to the brain. It is part of a survival mechanism without which fish could not have evolved.[11]

One of the fish which cascaded on to the deck of the trawler I sailed on was a shiny, darkly-mottled plaice the size of a tea tray, its bright orange spots gleaming in the sunlight. It wasn't gutted but tossed into a tray with other flat fish. After two or three hours I heard it literally croaking. A deckhand, witnessing my distress, nonchalantly clubbed it, presumably to death. Some eight hours later I looked down at the pathetic dead creature in an alien environment and was horrified to see its mouth and its gill covers opening and closing. Such is the tenacity of life and the survival abilities of plaice that it was still alive, enduring a suffocation which had already lasted over 10 hours.

As northern waters are fished out, species such as the plaice are giving way on the fishmonger's slab to more exotic types from all over the world, such as the parrot fish. In fact over 40 per cent of European fish sales are now 'exotics'.

Diving on the Malindi reef in Kenya and on the largest reef in the northern hemisphere off Belize, I've seen the undersea world from which these exotics are snatched. I have offered tasty tit bits and patiently waited while beautifully coloured parrot fish have found the courage to approach me and accept them. I have seen the tell-tale puffs of sand which betray the perfectly camouflaged hiding-place of rays and I have startled schools of dashing yellowtails into flight. It is a wonderfully colourful and fragile world.

But rather than learn from those practices which have devastated our home waters, Governments and corporations are exporting the same ethos to these delicately balanced ecosystems in the developing world. In the open seas, where no permission is needed, there is a bonanza of totally uncontrolled fishing where net size, fish size and catches are without limits. Humankind has never been short of ingenuity when it comes to killing, and the methods of catching and killing fish are no exception. They even extend to dynamite and poison.[12] And a new, even more damaging phenomenon has suddenly appeared called 'biomass fishing'. Nets of the tiniest gauge scoop up all living creatures in one destructive haul.

Where fishing grounds fall inside territorial waters, the rights to exploit them are bought cheaply from Governments desperate for hard currency with which to service their loans from Western banks. Those buying the fishing rights are often the same ones who made the loans in the first place and so the financial merry-go-round of dependency and impoverishment continues, as it has for decades.

One of the most damaging methods of fishing is the drift net. Constructed from thin but strong monofilament nylon, these nets hang down from the surface in what has become known as 'walls of death' and can stretch up to 50 kilometres in length. They trap squid, tuna and salmon, but also bring death to dolphins, small whales, turtles, seals, rays and sharks. Traditionally the favoured method of the Japanese and Taiwanese in the Pacific, they have now spread to the Atlantic and have been eagerly taken up by European fishermen as they start the search for new species. The posturing between Spanish and British West Country fisherman was over precisely this issue. Jingoism obscured the fact that these nets are responsible for the death of at least one million small whales and dolphins every year.

Another of the most obscene and rapidly increasing forms of fishing is 'finning', carried out by several Asian countries. Sharks have largely escaped being eaten up to now because their flesh tastes strongly of ammonia. Unfortunately their fins don't. So they are now caught in large numbers – estimates as high as 100 million annually are given by the Shark Protection League – and killed solely to provide the raw materials for shark's fin soup. They are dragged from the water, their fins are cut from them and they are dropped back into the sea to die from shock and drowning. These are creatures which have evolved for so long and so perfectly that they are almost free from disease. Their evolutionary success within their own environment is in sharp contrast to our own.

Meanwhile, as some species of animal are destroyed wholesale, others which depend upon them are reduced to hunger. Is it any wonder that more than 30,000 sea birds were washed up on the shores of the Shetland Islands in 1994,[13] dead from starvation, and for the first time ever there are recorded accounts of dolphins off the British coast attacking seals? It is thought they are so desperate for food that they have turned on other mammals with whom they have lived in harmony for millions of years.

As the numbers of fish decline, the demands by the fishing industry to eliminate the 'causes' of declining fish stocks grow louder. In 1991, the Russians shot 51,000 seals in order to 'protect' their fisheries and there are demands for similar culls in Britain. In 1995 the Canadian Government sanctioned the slaughter of 250,000 seals because of their predation on fish stocks.

In the meantime the overfishing continues. In the North Sea, only one third of all cod and haddock survive longer than 12 months.[14] Fish which would normally live for 10 years are being caught before they have even had time to breed.

The practice of catching immature fish has hit skate so badly that they have been exterminated from the Irish Sea. Their long life of 70 years or more and consequent late maturity has been their undoing.

In June 1995 the International Council for the Exploration of the Sea spoke out at a North Sea Protection Conference in Denmark. This is not a small fringe group without resources to check its science, but a body which comprises the world's official scientific advisers. ICES's conclusion is that the once teeming shoals of mackerel are now commercially extinct (i.e. too few to fish) and unless something dramatic is done, cod will become actually extinct (non-existent) within five years.[15]

The cost of all this destruction is another problem. According to the UN Food and Agriculture Organization, the value of the world's total fish catch is reckoned to be around US$ 70 billion, and yet the costs involved in running the fleets and marketing the fish is put at $124 billion.[16] The huge discrepancy between the two is largely covered by subsidies. Not only are the oceans being devastated, but every one of us is paying for it to happen.

Unfortunately this isn't the only problem. As a consequence of dumping sewage, heavy metals, pesticides and PCBs, mostly in northern waters, Dutch and German surveys have both found that around 40 per cent of flatfish are riddled with cancerous growths, ulcerations or skin diseases.[17] Researchers have also established that PCBs, amongst the most toxic of all substances, are now distributed throughout the food chain of the world's oceans. They are believed to have found their way into the fatty tissues of virtually every sea creature known to us. One of the effects of PCBs is to attack the immune system and permit diseases such as cancer to prosper.

In a separate piece of research by Greenpeace International, it was established that almost one third of fish eggs in the North Sea's main spawning grounds are malformed and more than half show abnormalities in their genetic structure.[18]

We are not separate from the world's food chain but integral to it. The billions of pounds spent on quilted lavatory paper and underarm deodorants cannot alter our status as just another animal. The PCBs which lurk in fatty tissues elsewhere also lurk in our own and the problem is more acute for meat eaters than vegetarians and particularly vegans.

The current answer to the overfishing problem is aquaculture – fish farming. But these intensified methods of production are no less damaging than the rape of the wild – and in many ways are dependent upon it.

One of the first species to be farmed was the salmon, a fish which has thrilled and excited us with its amazing migrations from ocean to stream and back again, so powerful and determined that it will leap over or swim vertically up waterfalls. What have we done with this wonder of nature? We have tried to breed out of it its amazing homing instincts and suspended it in netted containers in lochs and fjords. It is like caging swallows.

Dense population makes fish, like people, more vulnerable

to the spread of disease. Sea lice have thrived in fish farms and have spread out through the surrounding water to infect wild fish. In some areas, stocks of wild sea trout have dropped by 80 per cent[19] because of them. The toxic pesticide Dichlorvos, used to counteract the lice, is on the UK Government's Department of the Environment's 'red list' as one of the 24 most toxic substances used in Britain. Effective down to concentrations as 0.1 part per million,[20] it also wipes out crustaceans, shellfish and other marine life. It can cause cataracts in the penned fish and 55 per cent of wild salmon are also developing them.[21] A partially-sighted or blind salmon is not likely to fare too well in the survival stakes.

Of course, the lice have started to show a resistance to Dichlorvos, so salmon farmers are switching to another chemical called Invermectin, the effects of which are unknown.[22]

The sea-beds beneath the cages of fish farms and the surrounding areas are environmental black spots – literally. Faeces and uneaten food pellets form a sludge on which algae thrives. This can result in toxic 'blooms'. It is necessary to move the cages regularly – and subsequently spread the problem elsewhere.[23]

The awful irony of farmed fish production is their diet – food pellets derived from the slaughterhouse but also from fish caught in the wild specifically for the purpose. Try and work out the sense of that!

The finest indication we have of lack of concern for fish is the absence of regulations governing how they're killed. With farmed fish that is a huge number – over 50 million each year in Britain. The proliferation of ways in which stunning and death are dispensed shows imagination, if nothing else. Some are hit over the head with a piece of wood called a 'priest', a word and a method borrowed from 'sport' fishermen. Others are cut behind the gills so they bleed to death. Increasingly, fish are passed through a tank containing water saturated with carbon dioxide. One of the most popular methods is to take salmon from the water and immediately immerse them in crushed ice, where they slowly suffocate. This, apparently, is the best way of maintaining flesh quality. It also prolongs the consciousness, distress and suffering of the fish.

A study carried out by Bristol University's Department of Meat Science examined all these methods and found them wanting. It discovered that fish were often fully aware of what was happening to them even when they were lying still, supposedly unconscious or dead from one or other of these methods.[24] Perhaps if we imagine how we would feel being immersed in an alien world, where we can't even breathe, we can begin to empathize with the plight of these creatures who are so often dismissed as cold and unfeeling.

Across the world aquaculture is largely used to produce expensive species for which people will pay plenty of money – prawns, shrimps, trout, salmon, yellowtails. And the coastal areas chosen for the farms are usually the mangrove swamps, seen as useless areas ripe for exploitation. In fact they provide the most productive and important habitat in the oceans. Ninety per cent of marine fish rely upon the amazing diversity provided by mangroves, particularly for spawning, and over 2,000 species of fish, crustaceans and plants thrive there.[25] They prevent flooding, stop erosion, are the nursery of ocean life and are being ripped up faster than anyone can count. Indonesia, the Philippines, Malaysia, Thailand, Ecuador, Panama – wherever you look, clearance is rampant. The sub-tropical regions of the world have lost 70 per cent of all mangrove forests since 1960, largely to fish farming.[26] After a few years, the farms have to move on, leaving behind desolation.

As if all this wasn't enough, the reducing levels of ozone in the stratosphere may also have a dramatic impact on the oceans. The loss of ozone is one of the most worrying of many current environmental disasters. The Antarctic hole has been joined by a new one over the Arctic and smaller holes are appearing elsewhere. Not accidentally, I believe, people are encouraged to think that at worst all it will result in is a few extra skin cancers and cataracts. If only!

It is the greater concentrations of ultraviolet light which are penetrating to the Earth's surface which are the problem. It is known that increases of 10 per cent can kill anchovy fry down to a depth of one metre, but for some periods of the year the figure is already 40 per cent.[27] The real fear is that the increasing levels of ultraviolet will not only kill fish fry but also attack and destroy phytoplankton – the oceans' pastures, the vegetable base of its entire food chain and the producer of 80 per cent of the world's oxygen.[28] The consequences are almost unimaginable.

Chlorofluorocarbons (CFCs, used in refrigeration and foam manufacture) play a major role in ozone depletion but the enormous scale of livestock production world-wide also makes a contribution. Methane emissions from cattle and nitrous oxide from fertilizers, largely used to grow animal fodder, both produce ozone-destroying chemicals.

Even if there were concerted world action tomorrow, it would be decades before the effects were felt. There are now restrictions on the use of CFCs and PCBs, but in both cases they will continue to be released into the environment for possibly a further 70 years. There are no proposals to curb the number of animals. It is these delayed effects which ensure that we will have stepped over the threshold of no return long before we realize it.

If we as a species can create such a devastating impact in so few years, what on Earth does the future hold? Fortunately, individuals *can* influence the outcome and the easiest step you can take to distance yourself from this global nervous breakdown is to stop eating fish and other creatures from the sea. Simple really!

8 ◆ NOT SO FREE RANGE

Four years of campaigning with young people had worked and it now seemed the right time to broaden the approach and aim at adults also. I was appointed Campaigns Director of the Vegetarian Society and planned the organization's (and my) first adult strategy, 'Feeding You the Facts'. It was to be a five-month campaign culminating in National Vegetarian Day on 2 October 1991.

'Feeding You the Facts' was linked to a major survey I commissioned from Bradford University on attitudes towards animal cruelty and diet. It was the biggest survey of its kind and showed that several factors are at work when people make the decision to become vegetarian. For adults, nine out of ten stated that animal cruelty and health made them change their diet. Eight out of ten said that saving the environment and world food resources were also important considerations. However, vegetarianism was growing most quickly amongst 11 to 18 year olds and they singled out concern for animals as the most important reason by far.

Low down on the list of concerns for many people, however, are two animals rarely linked to stories of abuse – sheep and beef cattle. Seemingly these are the creatures most left to their own devices in a largely free range environment. I knew this to be untrue and set out to prove it.

Sheep are suited to the dry, rocky land of hill country, being prone to foot diseases when kept on damp lowland. Despite their inherent unsuitability for living on low-lying land, however, much of the Midlands has been given over to sheep rearing, as has Sussex, Kent, Devon and many other unhilly counties. The life led by these lowland creatures is considerably different from those reared on the uplands, such as in Wales.

The closest sheep to me is one solitary cade (orphan) lamb called Emily who is the pet of a local farmer's daughter. Emily defies all the ill-conceived judgements that you hear about sheep – nervous, jittery and distinctly stupid. She is bright, intelligent and behaves very like a puppy.

The contrast between Emily and the pathetic little creatures I saw on sale in a West Midlands cattle market was heartbreaking. A handful of them huddled together, shivering in the February cold, being prodded by prospective buyers blind to their plight. These frightened babies, no more than a few days old, selling for a few pounds each, are the direct result of an unbridled intensification in the sheep-meat industry.

Subsidies and science have allowed the size of the British flock to increase from about 34 million to 44 million animals in the decade up to 1992.[1] The UK is the EC's biggest sheep meat producer (about 350,000 tonnes in 1993), followed by Spain (250,000) and France (80,000).[2] However, more than 40 per cent of UK sheep and sheep meat was exported in 1993 as the British taste for lamb has been declining since 1989. As the market for lamb approaches saturation point, so the competition amongst producers intensifies and the price drops. Producers' overriding concern is to maintain the same rate of profit and the only variable in the equation is the sheep. So they have to be made more productive.

It is precisely the same process which drives down wages of human workers – the imperative to maintain profits regardless of the cost to animals, humans or the environment. It's called the free market, formerly known as capitalism, and it is a reality which those who care about animal rights, human rights and the health of our planet will eventually have to face if they want to change things.

The sheep which have fallen foul of this ethos would naturally produce one lamb after the worst of the winter has passed – in March or even April in the northern hemisphere. But as one producer tries desperately to steal a march on the others and sell at higher prices by offering the first 'new season's lamb', so the ewes are manipulated into giving birth earlier in the year – often in December.[3] An incredibly sick logic then switches into play – as they have given birth so early, why not get them to do it again? That is now the direction in which sheep farming is moving, producing three pregnancies every two years.

By the use of trickery, the ewe is deceived into ovulating earlier than she would do naturally. Contraceptive sponges are inserted into her vagina for a set period and then removed. Combined with doses of hormones obtained from pregnant mares, they provoke the ewe's body into beginning the process which would naturally be triggered in the autumn. When you add to the equation the squalid conditions in which the mares are kept tethered and immobile, the whole trade becomes a rather shameful and depressing tale.

Also, there has been a sudden glut of orphan lambs as a consequence of this rush to intensify production. Through all the usual methods of increased feed, selective breeding and the liberal use of drugs such as hormone implants, producers have turned the solitary lamb into twins and increasingly triplets. Unfortunately a ewe has only two teats and it is this which has led to the glut of orphans – this and an increasing number of dead ewes.

The old-fashioned way in which a ewe whose lamb had died was persuaded to accept an orphan from another ewe was rather gruesome but at least it was infrequent and involved no coercion. The dead lamb would be skinned and its fleece placed over the back of the orphan. With luck, the ewe would identify the smell of her dead lamb and accept the little newcomer as her own.

With the large-scale death of newborn lambs and the increase in triplets, such traditional methods have long since gone. Today, bereaved ewes are often forced into accepting orphan lambs by being held around their necks in stock-like devices while the lamb is put to their teats. The ewes can't move, they can't see the lamb that is suckling from them and the process can take as long as five days. It is probably exhaustion that wins in the end.

Over four million newborn lambs die every year in Britain, mainly from cold or starvation, some 20 per cent of all those born.[4] In Australia, sheep nation of the world with its 135 million animals, high rates of mortality are considered normal, with 20 to 40 per cent of lambs dying at birth for the same reasons.[5]

Most lowland sheep give birth in large sheds, being turned out to face the rigours of winter shortly afterwards. In upland areas, where the sheep are largely left to their own devices, they are under pressure for different reasons. Increased numbers of sheep are introduced onto scrubland where nutrition is at a premium, intensifying the struggle for survival. Human intervention in the form of shepherds is cut back and feed supplements are reduced. To meet 'market demands', efforts are being made to reduce the amount of fat on the animals through selective breeding and genetic manipulation – the one thing which helps them survive the cold when so much else is pitched against them. So it's hardly surprising that the highest proportion of lamb deaths takes place on the uplands.

Incidentally, one of the principal reasons offered by fox-hunters for their offensive pastime is the need to protect new-born lambs from the predation of foxes. This is a fallacy. Even MAFF has dismissed the problem as 'insignificant'[6] and in a poll carried out by one of the UK's leading 'sport' magazines, *The Field*, in April 1993, the 1000 farmers who responded to the survey showed that the number of lambs lost to foxes was only 1 per cent.[7] As ever-increasing numbers of lambs die from the cold or are born dead, however, the more winter-hungry foxes will be accused of being the culprit.

One thing about the farming industry is that it operates on logic – but of a very short-term nature. With lowland sheep-rearing, if the aim is to make ewes have as many lambs as possible and as often as possible, logic dictates that the easiest way to ensure it is to keep them indoors. And so the previously un-thinkable concept of intensified, high-density factory sheep farming is under way.

With this goes the whole panoply of medical intervention as the health of the flock deteriorates with diseases such as contagious foot rot and gut infection, prolapses, blindness, mastitis, rotting teeth and viral diseases. According to a leading veterinary expert at Bristol University, Dr Gerard Coles, 'The health of the British sheep flock is declining ... this is true for diseases caused by viruses, bacteria and ecto [skin] parasites.'[8]

It also involves the cruel invasiveness of forced artificial insemination, where the ewe is spreadeagled upside-down on a rack while the ram's semen is injected directly into her womb.

It requires the forced ejaculation of that semen by hand or by inserting an electrical probe into the anus of the ram, a pro-cedure which can afterwards leave the ram writhing in agony.

It includes the regular practice of sending ewes to slaughter when they are almost full-term pregnant – for the extra bit of cash which the weight of the unborn lambs adds to them.

Then there is the practice of mutilating young rams by attaching tight rubber rings to their tails (to prevent 'blow-fly strike') and their testicles so that both wither and drop off. Or they might both be sliced off with a knife without anaesthetic. If you challenge almost any farmer about the cruelty of this practice, they will laugh at you patronizingly and assure you: 'They don't feel a thing!' It has always been my ambition to find a male farmer who is contemplating a vasectomy and offer him my own, extremely permanent rubber ring version of the operation!

As to 'painless', even the UK Government's own Farm Animal Welfare Council doesn't fall for that one: 'There is no doubt that all methods of castration and tailing cause pain and distress.'[9] But they can do worse than that. If the castration ring is fitted too high it traps the urethra, making it impossible for the lamb to urinate. The outcome is inflammation, possibly tetanus, kidney failure and an extremely painful death. None of this is shown on Easter cards with their gambolling lambs. I think I might gambol if I had a tight rubber ring attached to my scrotum – if I had a scrotum.

Australian sheep farmers slice the skin and flesh around the sheep's tail with a pair of shears, literally skinning it alive, without any anaesthetic. This brutal practice is known as 'mulesing' and is meant to discourage blow-flies from laying their eggs, so causing fly-strike. Humane alternatives are available, but they take more time and effort.[10] Again, money wins the day.

There is an irony to all this which is galling. Some 41 per cent, or £521 million out of £1.2 billion in 1993/4,[11] of the income of sheep farmers in Britain comes from the public

purse, from taxation, from you and I. The Farm Animal Welfare
Council stated in its *Report on the Welfare of Sheep* in April 1994
that 'Most hill farmers and many lowland sheep keepers would
be incapable of financial survival if [subsidies] were
withdrawn.'[12]

All red meat producers receive Government subsidies of one
kind or another – subsidies for a trade which is damaging and
cruel and which we don't even need. Cast your mind back to the
days when coal mines were closed and steel works and ship-
yards. They were 'uneconomic' and 'undeserving of public subsidy'. But farming, now that's a different story. I wonder why?

But even with the huge public subsidies, meat production is
on the edge of profitability and so the ratchet of production has
continually to be notched up. That means even greater
intensification.

One of the most chilling sights I have ever seen was a shot
in the Channel 4 TV film *Jungleburger*, transmitted in 1987. The
airborne camera shows dozens of cattle grazing, but as the shot
zooms out you can see they are confined in a square with earth
ramparts. The camera continues to zoom out and shows
another, similar, square alongside the first, and then another
and another until the squares fill the whole landscape, stretch-
ing away into the distance in a huge, uninterrupted chequerboard – hundreds of squares containing tens of thousands of
cattle. They are 'feedlots' for beef production, a system perfected in the US, where there are 40,000 of them but just 200
contain nearly half the cattle in the States.[13] Of course Britain is
copying the idea and the first British feedlot was set up in 1987.
Big Farm Weekly reported in November 1989 that this feedlot
caused a public outcry when it carved up the Lincolnshire
wolds, on the grounds of animal welfare and environmental
damage.[14] The 2,500 cattle were kept outdoors all year with no

shelter or grazing. They were fed chicken manure and vegetable waste matter. After one year the local authority found the farm guilty on water pollution charges. Not an encouraging picture for the future.

The feedlot cows are given high-protein foods on the principle that it is easier to bring food to the animals than take animals to the food. It also makes it possible to rear more animals on a small area of land than grazing would allow.

Like sheep, cattle have always been seen as the most free and least interfered-with creatures, and for some that is still true. Suckler cows are allowed to keep their young with them, sometimes from birth until slaughter at two years old, grazing on open land in the summer and developing some of the normal maternal and herd relationships. But the UK is not a great producer of beef, importing most of its requirements from other countries, including Brazil, which grazes cattle on despoiled rainforest land.

Around two thirds of the beef we do 'grow' in the UK, like veal, is a by-product of the dairy industry.[15] According to MAFF, between 20 and 25 per cent of dairy cows need to be replaced each year, yet each cow produces a calf every year. There is obviously a super-abundance of calves.

Some of the cows will probably have been made pregnant with the semen of a bull with strong milk-producing genes, while for the remainder it will have been taken from a beef bull. This requires a series of judgements when the calves are born.

Female calves that resemble their milking mothers may be kept to replenish the herd; others that resemble the beefier male may be kept or sold on for low-quality beef products. Similarly with the male calves, those that resemble their mother will be destined for the Continental veal crates, while those that are beefier will be castrated to become beef bullocks.

In all cases they will be separated from their mothers as soon as they have drawn off the disease-preventing colostrum from her udders and the milk supply proper has started. Herds of orphan beef calves will be grazed together. Increasingly, however, they are being kept in large sheds, crammed together, dehorned and kept on concrete or slatted floors. The only reason why beef lots are not widespread appears to be the poor quality of the beef produced in the UK.

However, modern scientists are not to be defeated and the old devil logic comes into play again. If the reproductive rate of cows can't be increased, then increase the size of the calf! This has been achieved in Belgian Blue cattle by introducing a double-muscling gene which has the great advantage of increasing muscle growth in the rear of the cow, the part which contains most of the prime cuts and where the money is made. With all gene games, however, there is usually a *quid pro quo* and in the case of the Belgian Blue it is a reduction in the size of the pelvis and a narrowing of the pelvic canal. The result is that heifers can often no longer give birth naturally and are condemned to a lifetime of Caesarean sections, perhaps as many as 10.

Just as in humans, repeatedly cutting open the abdominal cavity is bound to become a painful and distressing process. With each subsequent incision, the scar tissue becomes thicker and proves more reluctant to heal. Professor John Webster, Head of the Department of Animal Husbandry at Bristol University, is in no doubt about its effects:

> Although a Caesarean section may prove less painful at the time than a natural birth, there are the questions of recovery from the fairly radical surgery of the abdominal cavity. There is also the high probability of producing adhesions within the cavity following repeated

surgery. And by analogy with humans, abdominal adhesions are very painful indeed.[16]

However, research is still continuing. Professor Peter Street, Head of the Department of Agriculture at Reading University, has pioneered the process of taking eggs from a high quality cow at the abattoir, fertilizing them in a test tube with semen from a selected beef bull and then implanting the resultant embryos in a surrogate cow mother under epidural anaesthetic. As he sees it:

> The problem with cattle in general is that they have one calf a year, which means that you have to spread a very heavy overhead reproductive cost over one unit of calf production. Now, if by implanting more than one embryo we can increase the litter size so from time to time we get two calves, then we're halving the reproductive overhead cost, so that is major efficiency in livestock production.[17]

By this method, low-quality cows, possibly near the end of their lives, can bear two prime beef calves. If, of course, the cow is unable to give birth naturally to the heavyweight twins, there is no great loss to the farmer if the delivery is by Caesarean section and the mother killed. It is a rapidly growing system, with some 14,000 cows being impregnated in this way in 1991,[18] and is heralded as a breakthrough:

> In effect, with this implanted, designed embryo, if we are able to manipulate the feeding system, we can design the whole carcass from embryo to plate to meet a particular market niche. The challenge for the agricultural sector is to produce for the food industry raw

material which is of constant specification so that
when they cut it up, pack it, put it through their cooking
regimes, or quality control regimes, or portion preparation regimes, they get predictable yields of product
which are brandable and give constant eating quality.[19]

Yet there are those of us who believe the fundamental concern
of anyone who works with animals should be to safeguard their
welfare and avoid all possible pain and suffering. It is we who
have taken them from the wild, who have destroyed their
habitat and through manipulation of their genes turned them
into unviable travesties of living creatures. What we are doing to
these animals in order 'to meet a particular market niche' is, I
believe, dehumanizing and brutalizing, both to those responsible and to those who relish the 'constant eating quality' but
ignore the pain in which their pleasure is conceived.

No, it isn't all sunlit summer meadows for either cows or
sheep – but then, you didn't really expect it to be, did you?

9 ◆ TRANSPORTS OF DESPAIR

There is always a danger of becoming inured to abuse through constant repetition, but some sights and sounds stay with you, haunting and troubling, confirming your belief that an absence of compassion is an absence of humanity. There is nothing which typifies this more than the transportation of animals. Extraordinarily, their status under the Treaty of Rome is exactly the same as that of tins of peas, machinery or bricks – they are nothing more than goods. All credit is due to Sir Andrew Bowden, who laid down a parliamentary motion in 1995 calling on the Government to reclassify them as sentient beings. The motion wasn't given enough parliamentary time and so fell.

One immediate effect of the 1995 demonstrations against live exports was to get European agriculture ministers to introduce a series of regulations covering journey times. However, all it did was to legalize the existing practices.

At the time this agreement was reached, not one official inspection had ever been made on transporter lorries throughout the whole of Europe, but reports and film footage had shown me exactly what is involved in the movement of animals. It is a depressing story of overcrowded lorries, journey times of up to 50 hours or more and animals dying of thirst and heat stroke or from being crushed and trampled underfoot. There is no happy ending for these animals, no return ticket – simply a one-way journey to death.

I have seen sheep punched repeatedly in the face with full force because they showed the slightest resistance when being unloaded. I have seen pigs, afraid of jumping the two metres from an upper tier of a lorry, have their feet and heads stamped on and kicked – and I have seen the broken legs that resulted. I have seen boars have their snouts broken with an iron bar because they bit each other out of fear at the overcrowding. I have watched pigs incapable of walking because of smashed legs being beaten, kicked and dragged into the slaughterhouse and others, with their intestines issuing from their anuses, being similarly driven to their deaths.

The abuses which occur throughout Europe are usually dismissed by British and European politicians as isolated incidents. This is, of course, disingenuous to say the least. So little effort is made to check on the conditions in transit that the bodies charged with responsibility cannot have a clue what really happens. In the total absence of inspection on the Continental mainland, such denials of abuse can be little more than cynical, knee-jerk reactions. With no fear of detection or censure, it could also explain why incidents of the most barbaric cruelty are widespread and commonplace amongst transporters.

In 1994, a film was released showing the fate of cattle exported from the EU to the Middle East.[1] By the time they reach Romania, the animals are so exhausted they are too weak to stand. A chain is shacked around their horns and in this manner they are hauled up from a truck and dumped onto a quay for transhipment. While in the air, the skin on the head of one poor creature tears away from its skull, a horn breaks and it falls two metres onto the concrete. There it is left, obviously badly injured, like discarded rubbish, all day and night in winter conditions.

The same film reveals the plight of cattle being transported from France to Egypt. Even before they are loaded onto the ship, their desperation for water is obvious after 30 hours without a drink. Even after loading, water is still not made available to them and they have to endure a further 30 hours of what can only be the most acute suffering. Some become demented while others physically break down. On this regular voyage, sometimes 40 or more cattle die as a result of the conditions they are forced to endure.

In 1993, a particularly disgusting trade was revealed, that of pregnant cows. Their route was from Holland to Ireland via Britain and involved three road journeys and two sea crossings. In June of that year, in a consignment of 38 pregnant cows arriving at Harwich, 20 were dead on arrival.[2] The cause was thought to have been suffocation. In another shipment to Northern Ireland, one cow had to be put down immediately on arrival and several others a few days later.[3]

Before these events, in 1991 and 1992, the Dutch Animal Welfare Society and the British Royal Society for the Prevention of Cruelty to Animals (RSPCA) tracked eight consignments of pigs being transported from Holland to Italy.[4] Almost every journey lasted for more than 30 hours and once the travelling time was 59 hours. In not one case were the animals given either food or water.

There is a bizarre and brutal logic behind this maltreatment. Pigs make extremely bad travellers, being prone to travel sickness to such a degree that they can die from it. The normal, albeit grim, way of trying to reduce the problem is to starve the animals of both food and water for up to 24 hours before travelling. It isn't known if that was the case in these charted journeys, but it is likely. So, to the journey times can be added a further possible 24 hours of deprivation.

The same groups tracked two consignments of sheep sent from the UK to southern Italy. Neither consignment was given either food or water during the entire duration of the journey, which in one case was 44 hours and in the other case 47 hours.[5]

One of the worst incidents involving sheep happened to a consignment of British animals en route to Greece via the Italian port of Brindisi.[6] When the ship arrived at Igoumenitsa, 302 sheep out of 400 were dead, it is presumed from heat exhaustion. And if proof were needed that there is an inherent insanity at work, while Britain exports about two million live sheep to Europe per year, it has also imported live sheep *from* the same destination. It was a practice which began and, fortunately, ended in 1994.

As one consignment after another arrived from Poland and Spain, a continuing story of diseased, distressed and injured animals developed. The fate of the final consignment of sheep perhaps sums up the callousness of the trade. One sheep was dead on arrival and a further three had to be immediately destroyed. Another ewe had given birth on the journey and a second gave birth during her overnight stop. In all, 26 sheep were considered to be unfit to continue their journey and were slaughtered, including the two mothers and their newborn lambs.[7]

For what it's worth, there is an EU regulation which is supposed to prohibit the transport of animals which might give birth during the journey.[8]

The Republic of Ireland is also heavily involved in the live exports trade and has developed new markets in North Africa, in particular Egypt and Libya. Unfortunately it's not easy to obtain information on the welfare of these animals, but with sea journey times of up to 10 days, even longer in rough weather, it can be imagined.

Most of the animals which have to endure this journey are

cattle. In his book, *A Far Cry from Noah*, Peter Stevenson, of Compassion in World Farming, includes a letter from a boat skipper. Speaking from firsthand experience, he explains the process of travel sickness in cattle, which are physically incapable of vomiting:

> They are ruminants and digest their food by fermenta-tion. When they are exposed to extreme motion, the fermentation increases and the gas production in their stomachs becomes excessive, resulting in the condition known as bloat. The whole abdomen becomes grossly extended, they suffer acute pain, falling down on the floor as they are flung around from side to side, grind-ing their teeth, moaning and groaning in agony, unable to breathe properly, until after hours or days of the most terrible suffering, their hearts eventually give out and, mercifully, they die.[9]

There are two particular scenes which summarize human disregard for other life forms and which must haunt anyone who has ever witnessed them.

The first is the treatment of dairy calves no more than a day or two old. As already mentioned, as soon as they have drawn the life-preserving colostrum from their mothers' udders they are separated from her and placed in sheds.

Once you have followed the mother cow's eyes as she watches with alarm as her offspring is carried away, once you have listened to the bellowing of grief which follows its disappearance, you will never view the dairy industry in the same light again.

Traditionally, the bewildered calves are mostly sent to market where they are bought by dealers and transported to the veal crates where they will spend their entire 22-week life.

Standing with difficulty on slatted floors, they are unable to turn round or to lie down properly. They have no bedding, no companionship and are never allowed to chew grass or hay because it might turn their flesh from white to pink, the colour it was meant to be. They are fed on a gruel diet and purposely diseased, made anaemic, to provide white flesh for the 'gourmet's' dinner table.

These pathetic little creatures lick at their crates and swallow their own hair in a desperate search for solid nourishment. Offer them your fingers and they will suck eagerly, seeking comfort as much as sustenance. That is just one aspect of modern farming in which all carnivores play a part. And, it has to be said, so do vegetarians.

The other scene which has marked me, and many others, for life was the treatment of a young but fully grown bull, filmed by Compassion in World Farming and shown on national TV in 1992.[10] He sat on the deck of a ship's hold in Croatia, his beautifully big and curly head looking around in obvious fear and pain. His pelvis had been broken. The handlers kicked and prodded, but he was incapable of movement. One of them placed an electric goad on his testicles and delivered a 70,000-volt shock. The creature raised his head and bellowed a cry to rend the soul. And it happened again and again for over half-an-hour. Each time he tried desperately to rise, scrabbling at the floor with his forelegs, but it was futile.

Eventually, still conscious, a shackle was attached to a foreleg and he was hauled up and out of the hold and dumped on the quayside. Pained and exhausted, he lay in a heap, unable even to raise his head. A debate followed between the ship's captain and the harbour authorities. It was decided it was more profitable to lose the beast at sea. He was hauled again into the air and dumped on the deck of the ship, which then set sail. As soon as it was clear of the harbour, the bull was thrown into the sea. Whether he was alive or dead seems almost irrelevant after such treatment.

This isn't simply a case of nasty foreigners doing terrible things to innocent animals, but is an integral part of the meat trade and increasingly international. Whenever and wherever a camera is turned on the transport and slaughter of animals it always comes up with images to disgust. Cruelty is commonplace and anyone who supports this trade by eating meat is directly involved in it.

Also, although integration of laws has supposedly now taken place in Europe, it does not apply to the manner in which food animals are killed. There are scenes which have been photographed and filmed by organizations from all over Europe as routine treatment and which are sickening. Sledgehammers are used on horses, screwdrivers sever spinal columns and animals have their throats cut while fully conscious.

Through Viva!'s French associates, a Boulogne-based organization called Aequalis, I received a photographic and verbal report on the fate of a lorry load of sheep and lambs from the UK. It finished up in a field outside Paris where the 1995 festival of Ramadan was being celebrated. The animals were off-loaded and ushered into corrals where they were given no food or water.

Improvised wooden frameworks like gallows had been erected and pits had been dug in the ground and covered with iron gratings. Either one at a time or in groups, the sheep and lambs were dragged from the corrals onto the gratings, where men struggled to upend them. The sheep naturally resisted, although the lambs were much easier to control.

Having got them onto their backs, the normal practice was for one man to place a foot on the animal's chin while another cut its throat. Groups of children stood around watching, their vacant faces indicating that they had seen it many times before.

My contact timed the deaths, which on average took four minutes. There were no controls, anyone could take a turn and use any knife. Once dead, the sheep and lambs were hoisted on the gallows, gutted, beheaded and skinned.

Many more of these unfortunate creatures were crudely trussed up with rope and bundled into the boots of ordinary cars, driven to the Paris suburbs where they were killed in a similar way with kitchen knives in people's back yards. This is religious, ritual slaughter and takes place all over the Muslim and Jewish world, both officially and unofficially.

If the thought of back gardens being turned into uncontrolled charnel houses seems very foreign, it isn't. As Ramadan approaches, little tethered goats and sheep can be seen awaiting their fate in gardens all over Britain. Even when the slaughter is carried out in 'approved' slaughterhouses, the method of death is much the same.

My concern does not spring out of racism, far from it, but out of concern for animal welfare. We have arbitrarily decided which cultural and religious habits we will and will not allow to supersede our own laws. We don't accept multiple marriages, clitorectomies, stoning to death for adultery, public beatings or beheadings or the amputation of limbs for theft, but we do allow animals to be killed in an uncontrolled and painful way. It has to end and there are Muslims and Jews who believe the same, who strongly maintain that if you read deeply enough into either religion you will see that each has vegetarianism at its heart.

So just what is the scale of live animal transportation around Europe? According to MAFF, Britain alone exported approximately one million lambs and sheep in 1995. For calves the figure is about 550,000 and pigs about 150,000.[11]

The annual trade from Ireland involves approximately

370,000 cattle, about 300,000 sheep and some 150,000 pigs. Across Europe as a whole, the figures are huge – about five million sheep and goats, nine million pigs and over three million cattle.[12]

There is something extremely cynical about the British Government's supposedly moral stance over live exports. From the moment the public protests first began to grab the headlines in 1994, different Ministers of Agriculture adopted the position that, yes, they would like to ban live exports, but the Treaty of Rome forbade them from doing so.

In fact, under Article 36 of the Treaty of Rome, there is a very good case for banning the trade on the grounds of public morality and the protection of health and life of animals. Although the Government made use of this clause until 1993 to prevent the export of live animals to Spain because of the appalling cruelty in Spanish slaughterhouses, it refused to use the same Article to ban live exports generally. It has consistently maintained that to do so would put it in breach of EU law and it would be called to account in the European Court. But such an outcome carries no damaging penalty and to appear in court in order to test a law is a common and accepted method of clarifying what a particular piece of legislation does and does not allow.

The hollowness of this position was abruptly exposed in January 1996, when the Government publicly admitted that it was fully prepared to ignore a European law.[13] The cause of the rebellion was a new EU regulation forbidding the use of a drug called Emtryl to prevent wasting diseases in game birds. Breeders of pheasants and partridges claimed the ban would devastate stocks, reducing the number of birds available to be shot in the autumn and winter – including, presumably, those killed by the Government ministers who still participate in blood sports.

You might think it ironic that the first public transgression of EU law was motivated by the desire to take life and not to save it. Of course it showed that the Government never had any intention of banning live exports, whether it was legal or illegal to do so.

Unfortunately that isn't the end of the cynicism. The practice of politics is such that any exposé which might reflect on Government policy tends immediately to be denied, diminished or dismissed as untypical. However, there is now a huge volume of eye witness and video evidence to show that cruelty is an integral part of the trade in live animals. It is supported by a welter of research.

One study examined two groups of lambs in transit, one which travelled for nine hours and one for 14 hours.[14] It concluded that they needed at least 144 hours to recover from their ordeal and at least 96 hours rest before being in a suitable state to continue their journeys.

New EU regulations on journey times introduced in 1995 appeared to take little account of this and other studies. Even if the new journey times are better policed than the old ones – and there is no evidence to show that they will be – they will still cause unacceptable suffering. Lambs can be transported for up to 21 hours, including a one-hour stop for food and water, during which time they remain on the lorry. After only a 24-hour break they can legally face a further 21-hour ordeal. For sheep and cattle it is worse – up to 31 hours with a one-hour stop for food and water. Again, after a 24-hour break the process can be repeated.[15]

In 1986 Roger Ewbank of the Universities Federation for Animal Welfare reviewed the available literature and research relating to the transport of calves. He looked at stress caused by temperature variations, at the prevalence of hunger, thirst and dehydration, at the rates of exhaustion and the risks of disease.

His conclusions were forthright:

> Although calves are robust creatures, they should
> be moved about as little as possible. Calves should
> ideally be reared on their farm of birth or, if unwanted,
> be transported to the nearest slaughterhouse for
> immediate killing.[16]

This view was supported in 1991 by the European Commission's Scientific Veterinary Committee, which stressed that live transport should be avoided wherever possible. It added that the long-distance transport of animals was unnecessary in the light of modern chilling methods.

In 1992 it went further and said that the EU law requiring that animals be given food and water after 24 hours' travel was quite insufficient.[17] In 1993 it actually admitted that even these unsatisfactory regulations were systematically flouted. It concluded: 'Long distance transport in overstocked vehicles, combined with dehydration and starvation, results in very poor welfare and often in high mortality.'[18]

Despite the growing awareness of the fate to which animals were being consigned, exports from Britain increased dramatically over this period. The British Government has consistently adopted the high moral ground over live exports, claiming that British animal welfare is the best in Europe. The implication is almost that St Francis personally carries the animals abroad on his shoulders, tending to their every need!

In fact, MAFF has known for some years that its own regulations were being flouted and commissioned a report from Divisional Veterinary Officer Hugh Morris. It became known as the Morris Report and was completed in March 1994.[19] Morris unearthed several disturbing ways in which the rules were being circumvented and clearly spelt them out. The report was highly secret, but I was able to obtain a copy. It stated:

> There was ample evidence of serious malpractice
> existing in the area of exports dealing with calves for
> further production and sheep for further production
> and immediate slaughter. Serious deficiencies were
> identified in relation to standards of identification and
> examination of animals.[20]

Another section criticized both the complexity of the rules and
those charged with policing them, particularly LVIs – Local
Veterinary Inspectors, responsible for examining animals prior
to export and the only safeguard of their welfare:

> State Veterinary Service staff believed the existing
> instructions were inappropriately structured, complex
> and difficult to understand. Furthermore, LVIs have
> frequently made little or no effort to refer to instruc-
> tions issued by the Ministry.[21]

In a bizarre piece of privatized, free-market logic which
almost ensures the regulations are broken, Local Veterinary
Inspectors are paid by the exporters whose animals they inspect.
If the exporters don't like the bill or the thoroughness of the
inspection or its findings, they can arrange to have the animals
inspected elsewhere, by another LVI. This can lead to a touting
for business, a reduction in charges or a meaningless inspection
which doesn't inconvenience the exporter. Morris identified the
inherent conflict in this:

> There was evidence that LVIs are subject to extreme
> pressures from dealers, hauliers, agents and exporters.
> The introduction of the Single Market has raised

exporters' expectations of free trade, the pressures
consequent upon such expectations contributing
directly to the irregularities identified.[22]

The British Government, which claims to be the guardian
of farm animal welfare in Europe, responded by banning the
report. When challenged on its attitude to the report's recommendations, it claimed that it had fully implemented them. But
in January 1996, along came a *Dispatches* documentary, 'The
Veal Trail', on Channel 4 TV, which revealed the hypocrisy of
this claim.[23]

- It clearly showed that the supposedly strictly enforced
regulations governing the transport of animals were still being
flouted at every stage. It exposed the fact that calves only two
weeks old were routinely beaten and were shipped abroad when
injured or ill, and that such welfare requirements as limited
journey times and rest breaks were often ignored. Perhaps the
most worrying aspect was that the calves' one protection, a
veterinary inspection prior to shipment, was nothing more
than a formality, with 500 calves being inspected in less than
two minutes.

The documentary also exposed the Government's
claims that strict control is exercised to prevent calves from
mothers infected with mad cow disease (Bovine Spongiform
Encephalopathy, BSE) as a sham. Two untrained youths were
charged with taking the ear tag numbers of hundreds of calves,
which have to be checked against a register of infected cattle.
Secret filming did not show these checks being carried out, but
did show exporters being offered a discount on the charges
levied if they prepared their own paperwork. It's like asking
a poacher to report the number of pheasants he kills!

What the programme revealed was that all the abuses
identified by Morris were still happening and the victims were

the pathetic little calves filmed arriving at the Petham lairage near Dover. So dehydrated were they that some were unable to stand and literally rolled down the loading ramp, trampled under the hooves of other calves. Despite clear footage of calves which could barely walk and others which were diseased, in the course of the programme, none were certified as being unfit to complete the journey to the veal crates of Europe.

One of the final scenes from this programme provided a sickening reminder of why protesters refuse to give up on live exports. The time: three in the morning; the place: the interior of a dirty, dingy French veal farm. The calves are driven out of their crates with electric goads. After 32 weeks of chained immobility they are covered in excreta and can hardly walk. Each stumble and stagger is met with more electric shocks. They are herded through a dark and narrow doorway to where they are to have their throats cut. It does not pay to speculate on the welfare standards with which each one of these little creatures was treated as it met its end.

These were British calves, so we can all be pleased with the statement issued by the Government when it refused to appear on the *Dispatches* programme: 'All the necessary action has been taken on the main recommendations of the report to ensure that our high standards of certification are maintained.'

If this is what humans are capable of doing to newborn, innocent animals, then God help all of us!

10 ◆ MEAT TO DIE

My first adult campaign, launched in May 1991, gave me
some hope for the future. The media latched on to the Bradford
University survey findings which showed a rapidly increasing
number of vegetarians and as a consequence I was dashing from
one TV studio to another and juggling press interviews between
them. I felt that at last I had a national platform from which to
drive home information about the abject state in which farm
animals lived and died. In the weeks following the launch,
membership of the charity increased by 25 per cent and that
increased my hope.

I had little time to relish the result, however, as I knew
there was something else approaching which would obscure any
sense of achievement in a cloud of anger, disgust and despair.
An animal rights activist had managed to get inside a slaughterhouse and was bringing the results of his investigation to me. I
had already depressed myself by sitting through videos shot
inside abattoirs all over Europe and these were disturbing
enough, but what I was waiting for was unofficial photographs,
video footage and a firsthand account, and I hoped this would
reveal what I knew to be the reality of 'humane slaughter' in
Britain.

The slaughterhouse filmed was a small one in the Potteries.

The filming was carried out over a few days and it defied the official position that if irregularities do take place they are infrequent. Irregularities were commonplace.

Slaughter is achieved by cutting an animal's throat and it bleeding to death, but there are two main methods used to first render it unconscious – electrical stunning and the captive bolt pistol. Both are supposed to reduce the risk of unnecessary pain. A third method of carbon dioxide stunning is used to a lesser degree by some pig abattoirs.

Electrical stunning is carried out with an instrument like a huge pair of scissors with insulated handles and an electrical terminal on each blade. The terminals are clamped on the animal's head and, if low voltage, should be held there for at least seven seconds while a shock is triggered to render it unconscious. A shackle is then attached to a hind leg and it is hauled up and its throat cut – referred to as 'sticking'. This method is largely used for pigs, sheep and some calves. A different method of stunning is used for chickens, as outlined earlier (see pp.36–40).

A captive bolt pistol looks like an ordinary pistol but instead of firing a bullet it fires a small bolt which flies out of the barrel but remains attached to the pistol. The pistol is placed in the centre of the forehead and fired. Theoretically the animal will be rendered immediately unconscious. To stop kicking, a metal rod – the 'pithing rod' – is inserted in the hole, passing through the brain and down the spinal column. Again, the animals – mostly cattle and some calves and to a lesser degree sheep – are hauled up and stuck.

Gassing by carbon dioxide is used in a minority of slaughterhouses in the UK. In Denmark most pigs are stunned by this method. Scientists have stated that CO_2 is an unpleasant gas because it creates a sense of breathlessness,[1] causing distress and panic.[2]

Although the trade is regulated, the Government has been lax at enforcing the rules, allowing the abattoir owners to put their men on piece work – the more they kill, the more they're paid. And speed and concern don't mix.

Carla Lane told me a story of wandering down a narrow alleyway and coming across a partially opened door. It was the emergency exit of a slaughterhouse, but she had gone inside before realizing this. Penned, hock-deep in blood and filth, was a group of fearful and nervous little calves. They shied away from any sudden noise or movement and cowered together at the edge of the pen. Each time a slaughterman passed them he shouted, terrifying them, and walked away laughing. That was 30 years ago and little seems to have changed.

In the secret footage I watched, a young slaughterer pulled a full-grown sow from a group of other jittery pigs by its ears and tail and then leaped onto her back. Round and round ran the petrified creature while the youth rode her like a rodeo performer, yelling at the top of his voice. The nervousness of the other pigs increased, the pig being ridden panicked and the youth fell off her, got up and kicked her several times in the stomach, then applied the tongs and she fell to the floor. He only kept the tongs in place for about three seconds and after she had been hauled up by her back leg, she could be seen struggling. He was still cursing her when he cut her throat.

Other footage showed a similarly inadequately stunned pig, covered in blood from its gaping throat, shake itself free from the shackles and fall to the floor where it ran around looking for a way out. The strange noises it made I took to be an attempt at squealing. As its blood drained away it gradually fell to the floor, was reshackled and hauled back up to continue through the production line.

A consignment of lambs arrived and each was shackled, hauled up and stuck without even an attempt at stunning.

The cacophony of their bleatings pierced my heart. I knew that their woolly heads can reduce the strength of the electric shock and assumed that to be the reason why they were not stunned, but I later found out from the man who did the filming that this was not the case. A big animal, if still conscious when hauled up, can kick the slaughtermen. Lambs were too small to cause injury and the lack of stunning increased the speed of throughput.

A farmer arrived with a consignment of pigs and unloaded them into the lairage. Off-loading included vicious kicks, punches and curses – a display of what appeared to be hatred. He stayed to assist with the slaughter and rushed the pigs down to the stunning point, forcing them by their tails. They squealed particularly loudly because he twisted each tail until it broke. The slaughtermen laughed – it was what he always did!

In another part of the footage, a steer was penned and the captive bolt used on it. It did not break through the bone of the skull. The slaughterman cursed and tried again. It still didn't work. He tried a third time, but the bullock, knowing what was coming, wrenched his head away and the bolt went through the side of his face. Five more attempts were made with the bullock rearing up on his hind legs before he was eventually brought to the floor with a successful shot. All the time the slaughterman could be heard swearing about the state of his pistol.

Contrasted with this carnage was a moment of inexplicable and bizarre tenderness. One of the older slaughtermen kept an old and obviously pregnant ewe in the lairage, away from the slaughter of the other sheep. Only when they had been killed and their carcasses moved along the line did he bring the old sheep forward to the stunning pen, talking to her kindly and patting her reassuringly. Still talking in gentle tones, he killed her.

Over the years since 1991 and in my current research with Viva!, I've found that many scientific studies back up what was revealed in the footage. Millions of animals are having their throats cut while fully conscious.

Stunning is supposed to render the animal unconscious before it is bled to death. It would be a quicker, more painless death for the animal if stunning killed it outright. But this is not done because of an outdated belief that it is necessary for the heart to continue to beat when the animal's throat is cut in order to force the last drop of blood from the carcass to stop bacterial growth and deterioration of the meat. However, it's now known that the same amount of blood remains in the meat whether or not the animal's heart is still beating.[3]

Inherent in the current methods of stunning is the danger that the animal will regain consciousness before its throat is slit. A study in the journal *Meat Science* in 1991 showed that pigs are not stunned with a strong enough electrical charge, as 38 per cent given 100 volts recovered in 10 seconds and those given 75 volts did not lose consciousness at all.[4] The Ministry of Agriculture's own code states that at least 240 volts are required to stun a pig effectively.[5] This is extremely worrying, as the voltages used in slaughterhouses can be as low as 75 volts[6] and are usually less than 150.

The Government's Farm Animal Welfare Council found in its review of slaughter in 1984 that a high percentage of slaughtermen were not bothering to place the electric tongs on the correct place on the pig's head.[7] This means that the shock paralyses the pig enough for the slaughterer to shackle its back leg and hang it upside-down, but not enough to stop it being aware of everything that is happening.

Another study published in the *Pig Veterinary Journal* in 1991 shows that even if pigs are stunned at higher voltages in the right place, the time taken until they are hung upside-down and sliced across the throat is almost always too long. They have enough time to come round.[8] This means that millions of pigs every year in Britain can feel the pain and terror of their blood draining away.

It comes as no surprise that scientists have revealed a similar story with cattle and sheep. Research published in the *British Veterinary Journal* in 1984 on the slaughter of sheep exposes a disgusting state of affairs.[9] By studying 10,000 sheep in 40 British slaughterhouses it shows that it takes from 73 seconds to five minutes between stunning and the sheep losing brain consciousness.[10] However, sheep are generally unconscious for only 50 to 60 seconds. Simple mathematics show that the majority of sheep in Britain are suffering the same fate as pigs – a cruel and barbaric death.

A paper given by a researcher at a veterinary conference in 1992 highlighted that most calves are also fully conscious when their throats are slit.[11] Many calves are stunned with electric tongs, which only renders them unconscious for 18 seconds.[12] This simply isn't long enough to stop them coming round. Most calves are fully conscious for the 104 seconds it takes before their brain stops functioning, after their throat is cut.

Finally, adult cattle are mainly stunned with the captive bolt pistol. The Farm Animal Welfare Council states in its 1984 report that most causes of ineffective stunning are due to the pistol being placed on the wrong part of the cow's head.[13] It saw a considerable number of cases where the bolt had to be fired twice before the cow became unconscious.

A survey in 1990 visited 27 abattoirs and looked at almost 2,000 cattle being stunned. It found that 7 per cent of cattle were 'less than effectively stunned'.[14] This translates to 220,000 dairy cows and beef cattle being put through agony.

The problem with statistics is that they convey nothing of the fear and pain, the bellowing of terrified and injured creatures. It is no wonder that this wholesale, ritualized, authorized animal abuse takes place behind closed doors. If people were forced to witness the panic in the eyes of dying animals, meat eating would be in terminal decline.

There are other many things which go on in the world of meat which are completely hidden from view and under normal circumstances never come to light. It was purely by coincidence that I happened to meet a woman who worked in the meat preparation department of a supermarket in the summer of 1992. It was the matter-of-fact way in which she spoke about her experiences that shocked me as much as what she said. It also started me off on a trail of discovery which left me feeling more than a little sick.

The little conversational gem which began it all was when she talked about finding 'peppermint creams' in the meat. Naïvely, I asked her to explain what she meant. I instinctively knew I wasn't going to like what I heard. 'Peppermint creams', apparently, are the circular, pus-filled little abscesses which the workers frequently exposed when they were portioning up the meat into its different cuts. The normal way of dealing with them was to scrape off the pus, cut out the affected part and throw it into the bin – not the waste bin but the *mince bin*. That's when I knew it was time to investigate the state of the meat which passes as fit for human consumption.

It transpired that with a few exceptions, most supermarkets have little control over where their meat comes from and while some know the farms and the abattoir involved, most go through a dealer. Just as worrying is the lack of control exercised by big public institutions, often with some of the most vulnerable people in society at their mercy – hospitals, old people's homes, residential homes, schools. Almost three-quarters of them have no idea where their meat comes from or its history.

They also usually buy through dealers and have no way of knowing if the regulations governing meat hygiene have been followed.

As central Government increasingly cuts back on financial support to local authorities and health and education authorities, so the need of these institutions to economize becomes paramount and their search for ever cheaper meat intensifies. Unfortunately cheap meat often means poor quality, condemned, rejected, diseased meat. And institutional dumping is only the extreme end of a business riddled with deception.

The whole system of quality control is a shambles and the Government's response is to create yet another unelected, unaccountable quango (quasi-autonomous, non-Governmental organization). In this instance it is the Meat Hygiene Service (MHS), which came into existence in 1995. I carried out most of my research in 1992/3, prior to its inception, but from my conversations with its spokesperson subsequently, I don't believe that the standard of quality control has changed.

Meat inspectors, those with the responsibility for controlling standards in slaughterhouses, used to be employed by local authorities. With the setting up of the MHS they had the option of remaining with the local authorities in the environmental health department or transferring to the new body. Many of them chose to remain.

So, in 1995, the MHS had considerably fewer meat inspectors than previously, when it was already acknowledged that there were far too few of them to carry out their job effectively. I was assured by their spokesperson, however, that they were now more efficient and better able to monitor standards because they were centrally controlled – but if you can believe that a bureaucracy with its offices in York is better able to control the inspection of an abattoir in Penzance than the Penzance Town Council, you'll believe anything.

An animal can be declared unfit for human consumption for a variety of reasons – because of disease, contamination with antibiotics or medications or because it is a 'casualty'. An injured, casualty animal must have a veterinary certificate, essentially to say that it has not been injected with any medication for a specified period prior to the injury. Animals must have been free from specific antibiotics for a certain period of time prior to slaughter or they are rendered unfit for human consumption. If they are medication-free, the carcass, or parts of it, can be used for human consumption. No vet's certificate and the creature is declared unfit and condemned. The price with a certificate: in excess of £1,000 for a beef cow in 1996; the price without a certificate: nothing – just a trip to the knacker's yard and a pet food can. With those huge price differentials involved there is every incentive to try and cheat the system, and frequently those who try succeed.

There are three ways in which they set about it. The most simple is to develop an understanding with the local vet. A large farmer with several hundred head of cattle makes an enormous contribution to a vet's income. The old cliché that he who pays the piper calls the tune is as true in this situation as any other. All it needs is a weak or unscrupulous vet and a casualty cow, which should go to the knacker's yard, is passed as fit for human consumption.

The second stage of the deception takes place inside the abattoir. All meat passed by the meat inspector is rubber stamped on the carcass. Not exactly an example of high-tech quality control, as any high street stationer can make a duplicate stamp for a few pounds – and some have done so. With a system where there are insufficient inspectors working under pressure, it is simplicity itself to stamp a diseased or damaged carcass or one which has been pumped full of antibiotics while still alive. (More on the dangers of antibiotics later; *see pp.114–117.*)

The third way of cheating the system is by night slaughtering, when there is no one around to check the animals. This is one of the simplest ways of getting round the rules.

Some of these laws, which also include restrictions on transporting sick and injured animals which are too weak to withstand the journey properly, are not based solely on concern. When an animal is tired or ill or stressed from a long journey, there is a rapid increase in its bacterial levels, which can affect the safety of the meat.

Similarly with abscesses – the presence of 'peppermint creams' isn't just a cosmetic concern. They produce poisons and high levels of bacterial growth, often highly toxic bacteria such as staphylococcus and streptococcus.

Despite this, many of these regulations are almost unenforceable. They are framed in such a way that there is no serious intent that they should ever be effective. Their implementation falls to the local trading standards officers who, on top of all their other work, can only enforce the regulations by making random checks. These are time-consuming and almost completely ineffective, which means there are few incentives to do them in the first place.

Cosy relationships between hauliers and slaughterhouse owners, particularly for night slaughtering, means that unscrupulous dealers can weave in and out of the regulations without ever being touched. In a manner similar to the way in which some companies buy bad debts, some dealers buy casualty cattle. Knowing that they can pass the meat off as fit for human consumption because of their deals with the slaughterers, they can pay more than the knacker man. Everyone along the line benefits – except the consumer who eats meat which should have been condemned.

A Channel 4 TV documentary team, with discreetly placed cameras, was able to show the reality of this cheating and what it means in terms of animal suffering. I saw their film, *The Bad Meat Trail*, in 1992 and it revealed some of the saddest scenes I have ever witnessed – lorries with sick and trembling creatures, unable to stand, being prodded and goaded into movement, treading painfully and fearfully through ill-lit yards towards a brutal death; stepping through the blood and filth of other, previously slaughtered creatures; another lorry with cattle painfully and barbarically slaughtered on the farm, their necks gaping wide as someone had inexpertly hacked away trying to find an artery. Other cattle which, on inspection, were shown to have a kaleidoscope of diseases – gangrene, pneumonia, septic peritonitis – all destined to be killed and served as someone's dinner.

They also uncovered an equally cynical disregard for human health in the way in which meat is illegally used. Cuts condemned as unfit for human consumption and stained bright green to identify them as such have finished up in meat pies. Joints returned from supermarkets because they have started to decompose have been trimmed, washed and repacked as fresh lean meat.

The health risks of eating red meat have begun to filter through to consumers, but ironically most are still largely ignorant of this particular aspect of the trade. Combined with the risks from saturated fat, cholesterol, possibly BSE *(see pp.186–193)* and other diseases, beef eating should be restricted to consenting adults acting in private.

More and more people are increasingly opting for the 'healthier' option of white meat, particularly chicken. This is unfortunately like jettisoning arsenic in favour of strychnine. As Ian Coghill, Vice Chairman of the Environmental Health Officers Food Safety Committee said on Radio 4's *File on Four* in February 1995, 'We have reached a situation where chicken should carry a Government health warning like a packet of cigarettes.'

In food-processing plants where they work with red meat as well as chicken, the chicken preparation areas are often cordoned off from the rest of the plant. The work there is carried out behind glass screens in a kind of quarantine, just in case the bugs which thrive in and on chicken leap out and infect everything else. The healthy option, eh?

One of the most widespread of these bugs is salmonella which, according to the Government's Department of Health, infects one third of all chickens.[15] A test carried out by Birmingham University in 1995 by leading microbiologist Dr Laura Piddock, however, found that almost every chicken they examined was infected.[16]

The Government's position on chicken is simple, straightforward and largely true: proper cooking of the meat will render the salmonella harmless. What they don't say, but what the Birmingham test revealed, is that nearly all raw chicken meat, in whatever form, is covered with salmonella. When you take it out of its wrapper, touching it in the process, you have salmonella on your hands and are likely to transfer it to almost everything you touch. The tests have clearly shown how these transferred infections can rapidly grow and flourish, producing huge colonies of the bacteria on all kinds of surfaces. If one of them happens to be cold meat or dairy products, then you have the potential for a very serious, possibly even fatal, bout of food poisoning.

How did we get to such a situation where something as simple as chicken meat needs a health warning?

In fact, salmonella is in all farm animals but the main cause of the problem in chicken lies in the slaughtering and preparation process. After their throats have been cut, the conveyor system carries the birds to the scalding tank, described earlier. The temperature of the tank is kept at 50°C – which is ideal for loosening feathers but totally useless at killing bacteria, which survive to a temperature of just below 63°C. If the tank were kept at this higher temperature it would prevent cross infection but would strip the skin from the birds, making them less saleable.

The next stage in promoting cross infection is the politely worded 'evisceration machine', also already described, which literally scoops out the chicken's internal organs with a spoon-like object. A water spray cleans the most obvious debris from the spoon between scoops but does nothing towards sterilizing it.

Almost every other process along the line helps to spread infection from one bird to another until they all finish up inside their plastic wrappers, seemingly clean and antiseptic, emblazoned with 'premium grade', 'top quality' and 'farm fresh' – but not 'Danger, this could kill you!'

There is a meat inspection service in the UK poultry industry. Once again, it used to consist of poultry meat inspectors under the authority of a public vet, but under European regulations which came into force in May 1994, routine inspections are now carried out by plant inspection assistants (PIAs) who are no longer employed by the local authority but by the owners of the factories whose poultry they inspect.

It is impossible to identify a salmonella-ridden carcass so the PIAs are essentially looking for birds which are obviously diseased or damaged. On average, they inspect 10,000 birds an hour, or five every two seconds – sounds a bit like the new NHS. Even Superman and his X-ray vision would find this task daunting, but the PIAs do reject some birds (presumably they have to be minus a leg or bright orange to be noticed). And if they reject too many birds, the pressure on them to be less critical can be enormous – both from their employers and from their workmates, who are mostly on a bonus payment system.

Salmonella and other bugs blossom from the very start of the chickens' lives and are endemic in the faeces-laden sheds.

As a matter of course, the chickens' food is dosed with antibiotics which, in true Orwellian deception, are labelled 'growth enhancing'. They work by killing bacteria in the gut which are potentially harmful to the chicken. This allows other, antibiotic-resistant bacteria to flourish which are harmful to humans but which don't harm the host bird. Salmonella is one of them. Antibiotics have allowed this potentially fatal organism to prosper and the chicken-handling process has distributed it. But there are other, possibly greater worries...

The use of antibiotics is comparatively recent as they weren't discovered until the 1940s. As with so many other discoveries, the scientific world went into raptures. The drugs were liberally distributed to humans and other animals as a cure for every kind of infection from boils to tuberculosis. And to begin with they were amazingly effective.

In 1969, however, the first trembles of misgiving began to be felt around the medical world when a large number of cows died from infections which refused to respond to antibiotic treatment. The assumption was that the cattle had developed a resistance to antibiotics through being regularly treated with them. At this time the same types of antibiotics were being prescribed for humans and animals alike. The fear was that if cows could develop a resistance, so could humans.

The outcome was an enquiry headed by Professor Michael Swann which determined that humans should be given different types of antibiotics from those used on other animals. That has been the situation ever since, except that recent developments have begun to blur the boundaries in a potentially worrying way.

Reported cases of food poisoning in Britain have increased steadily over the last decade and stood at around 85,000 in 1995, resulting in around 260 deaths.[17] The number of unreported cases is at the minimum 10 times this amount – about 2,300 people suffer from food poisoning every day in the UK.[18] The numbers have not only grown but the severity of attacks has also increased. Of great concern is the discovery that the types of antibiotics which are effective in treating food poisoning have reduced in number and now, for cases when all else has failed, there is only one – Ciproxin.[19] However, its power is being seriously challenged by the widespread use of antibiotics in poultry farming.

Ciproxin is one of a family of antibiotics known as fluoro-quinalones and although it has never been given to animals, an extremely close family member has. This is a drug known as Endofloxacine. It has routinely been used in chicken flocks throughout Europe since 1990 to stop the spread of disease in the overcrowded conditions – and one in six of the chickens sold in Britain is imported from Europe.

An even more widespread food poisoning bug in chicken (and unpasteurized milk) is campylobacter, which in 1991 accounted for 350,000 cases in Britain alone, nearly half the total.[20] Only one death resulted, but the bloody diarrhoea, abdominal pain and exhaustion it produces are extremely debil-itating. Campylobacter has started to become resistant to the wonder drug Ciproxin, almost certainly because of the use of Endofloxacine in chicken feed. It is feared that what has been produced is a 'superbug'.

The problem has been felt more acutely on the Continent. In Spain, for example, 70 per cent of campylobacter are resist-ant to antibiotic treatment. But at least we in Britain have managed to learn from their experience – or so you would think. The Government conducted tests on Baytril, the British-licensed version of Endofloxacine, in 1995 and has passed it for use in chickens in this country. Their tests, they say, show there is no problem.[21]

Dr Martin Wood of the Department of Infection, Heartlands Hospital, Birmingham, does not agree. He treats patients with food poisoning and said on BBC2 TV's programme *Meat* in 1995 that 'Ciproxin is used most regularly and has revolutionized the treatment of food poisoning.' However, the creation of a resistant superbug means 'some patients will become untreatable and will die'.[22]

Fortunately not all Governments have acted similarly and the Swedish administration has adopted a more responsible position by banning the drug completely.

The miracle of antibiotics is turning into something of a nightmare as bacteria, through their mutations, develop immunity to them. An extremely worrying development is the appearance of a new form of salmonella, DT 104, and of E.coli 0157, both of which are killers and are on the increase. The options for treating them are running out as resistance to five main antibiotics has already been identified. E.coli is essentially found in beef and in particular processed beef such as hamburger meat and sausages. Salmonella DT 104, unlike other strains of the bug, is also found in most cattle products.[23]

Many diseases are now simply failing to react to any antibiotics, including tuberculosis, which is now at plague proportions in many parts of the world and has even reappeared on the streets of Britain, particularly amongst the homeless and the very poor. Another indication of the growth of superbugs comes from the US, where it is estimated that 60,000 people annually die in hospital from a range of infections which fail to respond to any antibiotic.[24] Mostly it was not the infection which was responsible for the person's admission to hospital which was fatal, but something they picked up while in there!

There is also evidence that antibiotics may have a potential for promoting some diseases. It appears that people with a history of minor sexually-transmitted diseases treated with antibiotics are more at risk from contracting HIV. The timespan before it develops into full-blown AIDS also seems to be shorter.[25] Disturbingly, a variant of the HIV virus has now appeared in cattle and a similar link with antibiotics seems possible *(see pp.193–200)*.

However strong this relationship turns out to be, the facts remain that meat eaters are routinely eating flesh from animals which have been given antibiotics and the number of occasions on which antibiotics can be used, sometimes for life-threatening situations, is reducing. Meanwhile, the number of food poisoning organisms waiting to infect humans is increasing, encouraged by modern farming and production techniques.

Nearly 95 per cent of all food poisoning cases arise because of infected meat or dairy products. A meagre 5 per cent are accounted for by vegetables or fruit and many of these are the result of contamination by meat or animal manure.[26] The reason why meat is more dangerous is our biological closeness to food animals whose bacteria are much more adapted to living in our bodies than are the bacteria of vegetables. There are, in fact, many diseases which we share with animals and are capable of catching from them.

As far as I know, no one has contracted a fatal disease from a carrot.

11 ◆ AN APPLE A DAY

For generations we have been brought up with the belief that eating meat and fish is synonymous with good health. During the Second World War, the Ministry of Food provided children with cod liver oil and malt free of charge and mothers would impoverish themselves in order to get a bit of extra meat 'off the ration'. However, there wasn't much to be had. The meat ration at the end of the war was the few ounces that 1s 6d (6p) could buy per person per week while the butter ration was 2oz per person plus 4oz of margarine. Cheese was limited to 2oz, as was bacon (or ham). Sugar was also on ration, as were sweets, while fresh fruit and vegetables were not. There was also not much fish around. Strange, then, that people increasingly look back with nostalgia to this time and talk about it as one of the healthiest periods of our history.

On the basis of this experience you would think that a simple correlation is in order – less meat and fewer fish and dairy products means a healthier life! It's true, but vested interests have purposely blurred that message for decades.

As a campaigner and now as Director of the Vegetarian Society, I was better placed than most to get at the truth, as I had access to much of the scientific research which showed conclusively that a vegetarian diet was healthier than one based on meat.

The publication which first opened my eyes to the wealth of evidence linking meat with disease was a book by Peter Cox. Peter's *Why You Don't Need Meat* (Thorsons, 1986) made the health arguments accessible and easy to understand for the first time. He goes into even more detail in his latest book, *Peter Cox's Guide to Vegetarian Living* (Bloomsbury, 1995). But health had never been the motivating factor behind my vegetarian beliefs. It took a personal tragedy in 1988 to make me re-examine that position.

The sister of an extremely close friend was diagnosed as having stomach cancer and the prognosis was saddening – only weeks to live. She had three teenage daughters and a very close family and the scale of the collective grief was enormous. The sense of injustice, of impotence and of disbelief was all-powerful. There was a need to apportion blame, to seek out a culprit, as if by so doing a magical key would be unearthed which would reverse the relentless progress of the disease. I was present when the surgeon was asked, almost imploringly, whether there was anything known about the causes of cancer. It was the compassionate but matter-of-fact way he replied that I found almost disturbing. One thing they knew for certain, he said, was that there was an inescapable correlation between eating meat and stomach cancer. Other factors played a part, such as stress and smoking, but there was a clear link with diet.

I felt as though a massive deception had been perpetrated, not by him but by someone, somewhere. I asked myself why this wasn't public knowledge, why it wasn't emblazoned across the front pages of tabloid newspapers, why the official line was still one of denial – and still is. The woman who lay dying had fed her family meat as frequently as possible, genuinely believing that she was doing the best she could for them.

Unfortunately I have now learnt to be much more cynical about the motivation of the Government as a result of my search for the truth about diet and health. Almost every political decision concerning agriculture places meat in the ascendancy. In May 1990, for example, the then Minister of Agriculture, John Gummer, declared in his speech at the International Meat Trade Association, which was reported on the front page of *The Times*, that vegetarianism is 'wholly unnatural' and explicitly anti-God:

> I consider meat to be an essential part of the diet.
> The bible tells us that we are the masters of the fowl of
> the air and the beasts of the field and we very properly
> eat them. If the Almighty had wanted us to have three
> stomachs like grass-eating cattle [sic; they have four],
> I am sure he could have arranged it.[1]

Meanwhile, an array of posters and expensive press and TV advertising, partly paid for by the Government-backed Meat and Livestock Commission, proclaimed: 'Meat to Live' – giving a pretty clear message in defiance of the truth.

In 1995, the propaganda continued, with millions of pounds being spent on the cloyingly sentimental advertising campaign: 'Meat – the language of love!' And the MLC is still going into schools with expensively produced materials, including an interactive computer programme based around four young people setting up in business to – yes, you've guessed it – open a hamburger restaurant.

None of the information in these promotions gives even the slightest indication that meat is linked with the two biggest killers in the Western world – cancer and heart disease. It also fails to mention the essential nutrients which are completely absent from meat. Confusion and public relations gloss are being used to obscure the truth for the benefit of vested interests. And it is costing lives.

In the *British Medical Journal* in 1994, the interim results of a massive piece of research were published. It is known as 'the Oxford study' and it looked at 11,000 people over a 13-year period with the simple purpose of investigating the health consequences of a vegetarian diet.[2] In brief, the findings were that vegetarians stand around a 40 per cent less chance of developing any kind of cancer, have about 30 per cent less coronary heart disease and have a 20 per cent lower premature mortality than meat eaters – in simple language, they live longer!

However, despite being one of the largest and most thorough studies undertaken, with unequivocal results, the Oxford study still states:

> The results do not justify advice to exclude meat
> since several features of a vegetarian diet, apart from
> not eating meat, might reduce the risk.[3]

That is to say, it's not certain what it is that's making the difference. It might not be something in the meat that causes disease but something in the vegetarian diet that prevents it. Also:

> Our data do not provide justification for encouraging
> meat eaters to change to a vegetarian diet. However,
> they do confirm that those who have chosen to do so
> might expect reductions in premature mortality due to
> cancer and possibly ischaemic heart disease.[4]

Then there is this little conclusion:

> Dietary change may be a key determinant of the
> reduction in total mortality. Current recommendations
> in most Western countries advise people to adopt many
> of the attributes of a vegetarian diet but not to advise

> excluding meat. This advice seems appropriate in the
> light of our results.[5]

And long live the status quo!

The fact remains that thousands of lives could be saved and incalculable suffering could be ended right now by advising people to change to a vegetarian or vegan diet – not tomorrow or next week, but now. There is a mass of other research to support this recommendation.

The study didn't look at the effects of simply cutting down on meat, but it didn't stop them from recommending that option as the way forward. There was no justification for such a recommendation.

Does it really matter if there is some hidden ingredient, some obscure nutrient which no one has identified, lurking behind the eyes of a King Edward potato?

In a letter to the Minister of Health in August 1995, a Viva! contact asked why, in view of current knowledge, they were not promoting vegetarianism and she quoted the Oxford study. The reply was fascinating. It said that the study had not made allowances for the difference in people's lifestyles and the fact that vegetarians are less likely to drink and smoke. Because of this, the findings were not particularly relevant.

In fact, the study did make allowances for this:

> In this study, the 40 per cent reduction in cancer
> mortality in non-meat eaters ... could not be explained
> by differences in smoking habits, obesity and socio-
> economic status.[6]

There are two conclusions that can be drawn from the Government's reply: either it is incompetent or it is wilfully misleading people over matters of life and death.

Increasingly, when I appear on radio or television, a nutritionist from a supposedly independent body is asked for an opinion as to whether a vegetarian or vegan diet is healthy. Their answer usually starts: 'A vegetarian diet *can* be healthy but…' In those few words all the doubts necessary to discredit it are sown in the mind of the audience.

The nutritionist is often from the British Nutrition Foundation, which is, in fact, not independent but a food industry body whose chairman, Mr David A. Tate, has made it quite clear, in the BNF's annual report, what he thinks of scientific findings which link cancer and other health scares to meat:

> Unfortunately, I do not believe that the future will see an end to the publication of views which seem calculated to give the impression that food is ultimately life threatening. Statistics and league tables of premature deaths from heart disease or cancer linked to some dietary attribute tend to omit a reminder of other possible confounding factors.[7]

BNF's members include hamburger giants McDonald's Restaurants Ltd, turkey producers Bernard Matthews Plc, the Meat and Livestock Commission, Mars Ltd, Whitbread Plc, British Sugar Plc, Cadbury Ltd, Coca Cola Great Britain Ltd, Trebor Bassett Ltd and Tate & Lyle Plc – meat, meat, meat, sugar, beer, sugar, sugar, sugar, sugar and sugar.

I give this account to illustrate the difficulty in obtaining accurate, objective information about food and its links with health. The vested interests are extremely powerful and use techniques polished to perfection by the tobacco industry. The health risks of tobacco have been known since the 1950s and it is now the biggest avoidable killer in the world. Yet little is done to deter young people from taking up smoking – not even the banning of all advertising – and you can't get more cynical than that.

So, just what is the link between vegetarianism and health? There is overwhelming research to prove that vegetarians are infinitely healthier than meat eaters and live longer. Conversely, there are no diseases which afflict vegetarians but not meat eaters. That's a pretty powerful starting-point.

In the 1940s, the prevailing view was that animal protein held the answer to health and the more you ate the better. Nutritionists have been backpedalling from that piece of misinformation ever since. Now, the 100 leading health bodies from around the world, including Britain's Committee on the Medical Aspects of Food Policy (COMA) and the World Health Organization (WHO), offer very different advice – cut down on animal fats (which includes meat of all kinds and dairy products) and eat more complex carbohydrates (bread, pasta, potatoes, rice), fibre, fresh fruit, vegetables, cereals and pulses.

The eminent British Medical Association clearly states in its 1986 report *Diet, Nutrition and Health*: 'Vegetarians have lower rates of obesity, heart disease, high blood pressure, large bowel disorder and cancers and gallstones. Cholesterol levels tend to be lower.' It goes on to say that vegetarian and vegan diets provide all the nutrients required for a healthy diet.[8]

Some of these bodies have got as close as they can to saying 'Go vegan' but none has had the courage to actually say it. Why? Because it would be rubbished by Governments and food industries who are simply not prepared to jeopardize revenues with such a radical piece of advice.

But still the myth about animal protein hangs on. Tell someone you're about to turn vegetarian and they'll immediately become an expert on nutrition: 'What about protein? You're going to be seriously short of protein!'

Let's be absolutely clear. Protein is important because it's responsible for growth, for repairing tissue and protecting against infection. Fortunately, it's present, to a greater or lesser degree, in most foods and those with high concentrations include soya products such as tofu, soya milk, veggieburgers and textured vegetable protein (TVP). It is in cereals such as rice and pasta, some dairy products including cheese, milk and eggs, and in nuts and seeds. Don't worry about protein – it is almost impossible to go short. In fact you have a much better chance of winning first prize in the National Lottery than you do of meeting a vegetarian or vegan suffering from protein deficiency.

Protein is made up of different amino acids and some foods contain all the body needs while others contain only some of them. Meat contains them all, while eating a combination of vegetable foods combines different amino acids into a 'complete' form. The different foods can be eaten over time and don't need to be combined in one meal.

Far from worrying about lack of protein, there's much more reason to worry about too much of the stuff – animal protein, at any rate. It can damage your health. The most obvious example is that of the disease osteoporosis. It is also another example of industry's misinformation – in this case the dairy industry.

Osteoporosis is a condition which results in a loss of bone mass – the calcium which forms bones is reduced and weakened by being excreted out of the body in urine. It can result in easily broken bones and what used to be known as 'widow's stoop', where the chin drops lower and lower, eventually touching the chest, while the back becomes humped. There is some truth in the name – osteoporosis, or porous bones, tends to affect older, post-menopausal women, the category in which, I suppose, most widows fall. Many will not even know they have it until they break a bone, but every year in the UK, over 50,000 women break a hip because of osteoporosis and many of them die. In fact more women die from this cause than from cancers of the cervix, uterus and breast combined.[9]

The causes of osteoporosis are complex and involve changes in the hormonal levels responsible for making new bone and absorbing old bone. Oestrogen is part of this balancing act and following the menopause less is produced.

In order to avoid osteoporosis, women are encouraged to consume lots of calcium-rich milk and dairy products. This advice ignores world-wide evidence. Eskimos have one of the highest intakes of calcium in the world, yet also have one of the highest incidences of osteoporosis.[10] For the Chinese, on the other hand, the situation is reversed – they have one of the lowest intakes of dietary calcium and osteoporosis is rare.[11]

The missing link is animal protein. Eskimos eat huge amounts of animal protein and their high calcium intake comes largely from fish bones. The Chinese eat comparatively small amounts of animal protein and almost no dairy products. There is a direct correlation between the intake of animal protein and a loss of calcium. The same link does not exist with vegetable protein. The process is complex, but what is thought to happen is that animal protein produces an acid overload which is neutralized by the release of stored calcium from the bones before being excreted in urine. The same acid overload does not happen when the protein is from a vegetable source.

Most people in the UK have heard of osteoporosis for the simple reason that the milk marketing industry produced a series of huge street posters which stated that milk could prevent it. This campaign played on people's fears, but milk, instead of being part of the cure, was part of the problem.

The real prevention, according to new US research, has nothing to do with the milkman. It identifies boron, a trace element, as being extremely active in preventing calcium loss. By introducing it into the diet of a group of post-menopausal women, their calcium loss was reduced by 40 per cent.[12] No boron is found in meat or in dairy produce, but it is in apples, pears, grapes, nuts, leafy vegetables and legumes.

A possible lack of calcium also often worries mothers when their children give up meat. Strange, since meat contains little or no calcium. Vegans get all the calcium they need from leafy green vegetables, pulses, nuts and seeds – particularly almonds and sesame seeds. Also, some soya products, such as soya milk, can now be obtained fortified with calcium. Vegetarians obviously obtain calcium from milk, but it is these vegan foods which are the healthiest and which discourage osteoporosis.

Apart from protein and calcium, it is often claimed that a vegetarian diet lacks vitamin B12. B12 is an important vitamin, essential for the development of blood cells and nerve function, and a lack of it can lead to a collapse of the nervous system and eventually death. However, the liver can store it for years and only minute traces are needed – the equivalent to one-millionth of a gram per day. So you can pig out one day and eat none for days after.

Vegetarians get all the B12 they need from dairy products, while vegans are amply supplied by fortified foods such as soya milk, TVP and most breakfast cereals. Yeast extract such as Marmite, Vecon and Vegemite is also a good source, as is the large range of yeast-based spreads and pâtés. Vegans do not need to take vitamin B12 supplements – or go on about them *ad nauseam*.

The vitamin is produced by micro-organisms such as yeasts, bacteria, moulds and algae and it is widely present in the soil. The reason why it is found in meat is because of the ingestion by animals of small amounts of soil containing B12 when they are grazing or rooting. It was in exactly this way that our ancestors obtained the vitamin, before the supermarkets started sanitizing their carrots and before a touch of soil in cabbage became reason for contacting the Environmental Health Officer.

In fact, every vitamin you need can be obtained from a vegetarian and vegan diet, while meat is lacking several of the most important. Even those it does contain are not necessarily of the right kind. Take vitamin A, for example. It is one of the important protectors against disease – but only the vitamin A obtained from vegetable foods. It is present in meat as retinol, which can be extremely toxic in high concentrations, such as in the liver of cattle, and can even damage the human foetus, which is why pregnant women are now advised to avoid eating liver. The vegetable version is converted by the body from a substance called beta-carotene, which is found in a wide range of fruits and vegetables. Beta-carotene, together with vitamins C and E, has such a huge and positive impact on human health that it ranks as one of the great medical discoveries and I'll come on to that later *(see pp.136–138)*.

Vitamin C (ascorbic acid) grows in importance the more we find out about it and its central role in the functioning of the human body and its immune system. We are one of the few species whose bodies cannot synthesize it and because we can't store it either, a regular intake is vital. Fortunately, it occurs in a huge range of fruits and vegetables, so vegetarians and vegans are better placed than most to get their daily intake. Interestingly, there is no vitamin C in meat and dairy products.

Other essential vitamins almost absent from meat are D, K and E. They are all present in a vegetarian or vegan diet.

Because Viva! has such a big youth interest, I am often asked questions about teenage girls and their susceptibility to anaemia due to lack of iron in the diet. The view of some 'independent' nutritionists is that meat is the best source of iron because the iron from vegetables is more difficult for the body to absorb and therefore adolescence is not the best time to change to a vegetarian diet. However, iron is present in a whole range of plants and is made more easily absorbable by the vitamin C in fruit and vegetables – something which vegetarians and vegans tend to eat a lot of!

The truth is that iron deficiency is largely a female condition, linked to menstruation and affecting one in five of all women of childbearing age, regardless of their diet. One of the most respected medical bodies in the world, the British Medical Association, categorically stated in their report *Diet, nutrition and health* that 'iron deficiency is no more common' in vegetarians and vegans than in meat eaters.[13] Research on British vegans by the Department of Biochemistry at the University of Surrey also concluded, in a paper published in the *British Journal of Nutrition*, that iron levels 'were normal in all the vegans' and that 'pregnancy in caucasian vegans and the health of children reared on vegan diets appear to be essentially normal'.[14]

Apart from natural loss of iron through menstruation, it is often a problem of absorption, for meat eaters as well as vegetarians, that causes a deficiency. Good sources of iron include dark green leafy vegetables, tofu, wholemeal bread, pasta, dried fruit, pistachio and cashew nuts, pulses (e.g. baked beans, peas, butter beans, broad beans, chick peas), fortified breakfast cereals, pumpkin seeds, hummus, lentils, sesame seeds, jacket potatoes, hummus, lentils, molasses, oats and cocoa (a good excuse to eat plain chocolate!) Remember to eat foods containing vitamin C (in most green veg., potatoes, tomatoes, citrus fruits and juice) at the same time for considerably better absorption.

Another big misconception surrounds carbohydrates. At one time they were popularly seen as the slimmer's enemy, one of the primary causes of obesity and to be avoided. That couldn't have been more wrong. Carbohydrates are one of the most essential ingredients of our diet.

They break down into three groups – simple, complex and dietary fibre. The least valuable are the simple carbohydrates – sugars found naturally in foods such as fruit and milk or as the refined version in table sugar, sweets and so on.

Complex carbohydrates are the ones that we are now being encouraged to include as the basis of our diet and they are entirely plant-based – rice, bread, pasta, pulses, wheat, barley, millet, oats and buckwheat. The other big source, of course, is potatoes – or yams, sweet potatoes and casava. Complex carbohydrates are the primary source of our energy.

The third carbohydrate, dietary fibre, is the indigestible part of all the different plant foods we eat. It contains no nutrients but is the vital element which allows the bowels to function properly, reducing the chances of colon cancer. With wonderful visual imagery, fibre is often referred to as the broom which sweeps the bowels clean. It puts a whole new light on the song 'Hey ho, hey ho, it's off to work we go…'! Critical to human health, it is another vital dietary component which is completely lacking in meat.

Fats and oils are another important part of the diet, responsible for repairing tissue, manufacturing hormones, providing essential fatty acids and carrying some vitamins. However, not all fats are desirable or necessary and the least needed and most harmful is saturated fat, the type found in meat (even the lean parts), lard and dairy produce.

Saturated fats tend to be solid at room temperature – such as butter and lard – and unsaturated fats tend to be liquid – such as olive or sunflower oil – but too much of either makes you fat.

Saturated fats are linked with a whole range of diseases, in particular heart disease and cancer, and we do not need them in the diet. Something else we don't need to eat is yet another product of meat, fish and dairy produce: cholesterol.

Cholesterol is a sterol and despite the bad press it has received in recent years, it is essential for life. It is used for making cell walls, hormones, vitamin D and bile acids, but we don't need to eat it. It is manufactured by the liver and intestinal cells and, according to a growing number of medical authorities, no other source is necessary.[15] In fact, eating foods high in cholesterol and saturated fats increases blood cholesterol to dangerous levels. Excess cholesterol furs up the arteries, which can eventually lead to a total blockage which cuts off the blood supply. If the arteries supplying the heart are blocked, a heart attack is the result; if the arteries supplying the brain are blocked, you suffer a stroke. Cholesterol levels are considerably lower in vegetarians.[16]

Gallstones are another problem. Made mainly of solidified cholesterol, they can lead to inflammation and gangrene of the gall bladder, causing great pain. *The British Medical Journal* states that gallstones occur twice as frequently in meat eaters as in vegetarians.[17]

As we in the West have elevated meat eating almost to a religion and the majority of the rest of the world, for reasons of culture or poverty, simply doesn't eat meat on anything like the same scale, we provide an excellent human laboratory. We, the privileged, the principal users of the world's resources and consumers of animal flesh, account for only one fifth of the world's population, yet we have a half of all the world's cancers.[18] One in three of us will be diagnosed as having cancer at some time in our lives. And the situation is worsening.

A huge amount of time and money has been spent in trying to find an explanation for this disturbing statistic and, if possible, develop a cure. In a commercial world, a cure which involves a pill, a potion or a treatment is always preferable to a change in lifestyle, because pills can be patented, packaged and sold. However, not only has the magical cure proved elusive, but also the search for it has blinded people to the way in which they can take control of their own lives and reduce their own risks.

The Oxford study finding that vegetarians get 40 per cent fewer cancers was only one of many studies from around the world which have come to similar conclusions. They provide a huge incentive to take up a vegetarian – or, better still, vegan – diet because all the evidence is now one way, building a conclusive picture of animal protein as a cause of cancer.

Every five years, the US Government's *Dietary Guidelines* are revised and in 1995, the Physicians Committee for Responsible Medicine (PCRM) made representation to the Federal Advisory Committee, the body charged with the task.[19] As part of their submission that a vegetarian diet is important in reducing the risk of many diseases, they carried out a review of research and published work from around the world. Their findings were little short of staggering.

They found that the cancer rate amongst vegetarians is between 25 and 50 per cent lower than in the general population. Like any serious study, they took account of lifestyles – drinking, smoking, exercise, body weight – and compared like with like.[20] In a country where 1.2 million people are diagnosed with cancer every year and 526,000 die of it,[21] the implications of this are enormous. A national change to a vegetarian diet could result in a reduction of over 250,000 deaths annually from this one disease alone. The economic implications are almost as awesome – a halving of the $35 billion direct medical costs for treating cancer.

An important feature of this detailed research was the discovery that the increased consumption of fruit and vegetables common in a vegetarian diet makes a big contribution to reducing risks. However, it doesn't fully account for it.[22] The implication is that while a vegetarian diet does have great health benefits, there is something in a meat-based diet which actually increases the risk of cancer.

The benefits of vegetarianism are just as great with that other huge epidemic – heart disease. It is now the number one killer in the industrialized world and Britain is the capital of it. One in three men and one in four women will die of it – 468 of them every 24 hours.[23] The evidence is so overwhelming that vegetarians, and particularly vegans, are so much less at risk that their diets should be available on the NHS. One study, published in the *American Journal of Clinical Nutrition*, which looked at nearly 5,000 British vegetarians over seven years, found them to be 50 per cent less at risk from heart disease than meat eaters.[24] A study of lifelong vegans, this time published in the *British Medical Journal*, came up with a figure of 57 per cent less risk.[25]

In the United States the problem is hardly less acute. Approximately one million people have a heart attack every year, 45 per cent of whom are under 65.[26] Again, there are enormous economic implications for this epidemic, with the direct medical costs amounting to $40 billion. The cost in pain, discomfort, fear and grief is, of course, incalculable.

In their submission to the US Government, the PCRM also examined the link between heart disease and vegetarianism by reviewing the available literature. Their findings are again little short of astonishing. Vegetarians, they discovered, are between 25 and 50 per cent less likely to die of heart disease than meat eaters. Again, all the studies compare like with like.[27]

Part and parcel of coronary heart disease, as well as stroke and cerebral haemorrhage, is of course atherosclerosis – clogged up arteries. And here again the link with meat is indisputable. The good news is that a low-fat, vegetarian diet helps to reverse it. It also helps with hypertension, or high blood pressure, which makes the heart work harder to pump blood around the body.

A Swedish study, based on the simple premise of substituting the meat-based diet of those with hypertension for a strict vegan diet, produced some amazing results.[28] At the end of the trial period they found that of the 26 patients, 20 had given up their medication entirely and six had reduced their medication – mostly by half. Fifty per cent felt much 'better' and 30 per cent said they felt 'completely recovered'. Blood cholesterol levels dropped by an average of 15 per cent and health authorities estimated their savings on drugs and hospitalization at £1,000 per patient.

In 1990, what must be considered a medical breakthrough took place with a study specifically structured to evaluate the effect of a vegan diet on reversing the effects of clogged up arteries in coronary heart disease. Two groups were studied, the first being placed on a diet of fruit, vegetables, grains, legumes and soya bean products, and the second, control group, continuing with their usual diet. The extent of the arterial blockages was measured in both groups. After one year, the blockages of 18 of the 22 people on the vegan diet had reduced in size, while the blockages of two thirds of the control group had increased.[29] Subsequent studies have confirmed this extraordinary result – that damage caused by coronary heart disease can be reversed simply through diet.

The studies quoted here relating to cancer and heart disease are only a small selection of a huge and increasing volume of evidence which consistently points to a vegetarian diet as being the prerequisite for good health.

In 1989, initial results were announced from a huge study which looked at real people in real life situations. Its findings were so conclusive that you would have thought the world could not ignore it. A combined Chinese–British–American effort, it looked at the health and eating habits of 6,500 Chinese and became known as the China study.[30] Headlines in the *New York Times* on 8 May of that year summed up its findings: 'Huge Study of Diet Indicts Fat and Meat'. In short, it found that the greatest single influence on the growth of degenerative diseases such as coronary heart disease, cancer and diabetes seemed to be the amount of animal protein eaten – the more you eat, the greater your risk.

In an interview in the *New York Times*, also on 8 May, Dr T. Colin Campbell, of Cornell University, who was in charge of the American contribution, summed up his feelings on the findings: 'We're basically a vegetarian species and should be eating a wide variety of plant foods and minimizing our intake of animal foods.'

We're left with the question of why, if giving up meat is so effective, do Governments still steer clear of endorsing it? The answer lies within the power structures of society and industry.

In the US, the power of the National Rifle Association (NRA) is legendary and it has consistently managed to thwart any legislation which even hints at controlling firearms. The power of the livestock industry – and in the US that means the beef industry – is considered by many to be only second to the NRA. The clear link between ill health and meat eating has been so comprehensively ignored that up until 1995 the US *Dietary Guidelines*, which outline those foods which should be eaten to promote good health and those which are optional, made no mention of vegetarianism. It is the opinion of the PCRM that effective lobbying by meat interests was responsible for this.

The PCRM's submission to the US Government was accompanied by a request to remove meat from the obligatory category and place it in the optional category. They didn't succeed, but at least the *Dietary Guidelines* do now contain an extremely strong reference to vegetarianism:

> ...lacto-ovo vegetarians enjoy excellent health. Vegetari- an diets are consistent with the *Dietary Guidelines* and can meet Recommended Daily Allowances for nutrients. Protein is not limited in vegetarian diets...[31]

This is seen as a victory by the PCRM and a first and important step in establishing the enormous health advantages of a vegetarian diet.

In varying degrees, vegetarians are less likely to develop 60 or more diseases which, apart from those already mentioned, include asthma, angina, arthritis and rheumatism, constipation, diabetes, eczema, psoriasis and obesity.

So what is it about a plant-based diet that reduces the risk of disease and prolongs life? Low saturated fat and high fibre play a part and recent research has identified three other important ingredients. They are all vitamins and have been termed 'antioxidants'.

You will know that rust can eat the paint off a car. That damage is caused by oxidation. A similar process harms the cells of your body. In fact, it is at least partly responsible for dozens of diseases.

Unless you have discovered how to live without breathing, you cannot escape the consequences of oxidation. It takes place whenever oxygen combines with another substance, as when you burn food for energy. You need oxygen, of course, for the same reason a car needs it – to help burn fuel for energy or power.

Whenever you breathe, exercise or digest food, your body produces potentially harmful agents called 'free radicals'. Not a political group, free radicals are unstable molecules made by your body. In stable molecules, electrons usually associate in pairs. Normal body functions, however, can remove one electron in a pair. The remaining molecule with an unpaired electron is a free radical. The free radical tries to regain an electron and does so by snatching one from another molecule. This only creates another free radical, sparking a catastrophic chain reaction that eats away at your cells and damages the genetic material inside them. As stated by a nutritionist at the Solgar Nutritional Research Centre: 'Imagine if someone scrambled all the area codes in your telephone book; all your calls would result in wrong numbers. In the same fashion, jumbled genetic codes in your cells make you vulnerable to any one of the sixty different serious physical illnesses.'[32]

The free radical process takes place all the time, but cigarette smoke, air pollution, ultraviolet light and emotional stress generate more. You'll be relieved to hear that a vegetarian/vegan diet is a powerful ally in the fight against free radicals, because it contains a high number of antioxidants.

This newly discovered vitamin triumvirate (along with trace elements such as selenium and zinc) neatly mops up the out of control molecules and protects our cells against them. The three vitamins are the beta-carotene form of vitamin A, and vitamins C and E – none of which are in meat. But the number of different plant foods which contains them is enormous.

Vitamin C is in a whole range of fresh fruit and veg., but particularly citrus fruits, potatoes, tomatoes, cabbage and spinach. Beta-carotene is found in green, yellow and orange fruits and in vegetables such as broccoli, carrots and lettuce. Vitamin E is in most vegetable oils, nuts and seeds, avocado pears, olives, wholemeal bread, wheatgerm, garlic, dark green leafy vegetables, margarine, milk, butter and onions.

The implications of this dramatic discovery are only really just beginning to sink in, but it will eventually make it progressively more difficult for the meat interests to continue to spread confusion. In the past meat marketers have been allowed a total freedom, unrestrained even by truth. We are now involved in the massive task of slowly unpicking the web of deceit and misinformation which has been woven. We can then start to improve the health of the nation and reduce animal suffering.

By the way, if you have wondered why doctors haven't joined in this condemnation of meat eating, in fact still tend to promote meat, then here's your answer. Of the six or more years of training undertaken by UK doctors, nutrition accounts for only one day. In the US it is 2.5 hours – and they are optional.

12 ◆ APING THE PAST

My own research had left me in no doubt that we are naturally vegan, but many people still insist that we are meant to eat meat and as proof quote the fact that some chimpanzees eat it. This revelation came in a David Attenborough film in which one particular group of chimpanzees actively chased and caught colobus monkeys. We also know that other chimps will push sticks into termite heaps and eat the insects which adhere to the stick when it's pulled out again.

Fortunately, Jane Goodall, the scientist who devoted so much of her life to observing chimps in the wild, was able to document faithfully the eating habits of these supposedly carnivorous apes. Over a 10-year period, the group of about 50 chimps killed and ate 95 small animals, usually the young of bush buck, bush pigs or baboons. There was no concerted attempt to hunt them, simply an accidental stumbling upon them. The total daily intake of meat for each chimp was about 2.4 grams – the size of a pea, which is equivalent to eating an 85-gram hamburger once a month.

Other apes have been seen eating insects, in particular rotten fruit containing insects, but this is believed to have much more to do with the sweet taste than any inherent bloodlust for meat. There is no record of any apes searching out frogs, lizards and invertebrates on the forest floor, which would be the easiest way of acquiring meat if that was their desire. The main point remains that nearly all the great apes, some 80 per cent, are vegetarian – vegan, in fact. Any meat that individual groups may have eaten has not been sufficient to change them in evolutionary terms.

Every species of ape is equipped with a body designed to cope with an herbivorous, vegan diet: grasses, leaves, nuts, berries, fruits and roots, probably seeds and stems, bulbs and possibly lichen or the algae from ponds. Cambium, the soft layer on trees which swells beneath the bark in spring to carry nutrients, is known to have been an important food for apes – and we still eat it but call it slippery elm.

If you compare the teeth of an ape with those of a carnivore, or even an omnivore such as a pig or a bear, there is little resemblance. Apes' teeth include small canines and molars which have a large grinding surface with a thick covering of enamel – pretty much like our own. The jaw hinge is not fixed, able only to open and close in a cutting motion as with carnivores, but is movable, enabling the teeth to slide from side to side in a powerful crushing and grinding motion. This is all part of the need to begin digestion of tough vegetable foods in the mouth prior to it even entering the stomach. Carnivores, on the other hand, bolt their food in mouthfuls, relying on the much more powerful stomach acids to perform the task of digestion.

The US general practitioner and vegan Michael Klaper makes the point beautifully. In his talks on veganism and health he suggests that if you think you are naturally meant to eat meat, try running out into a field, jumping on the back of a cow and biting it. Neither our teeth nor our nails would even penetrate its skin.

There's no reason why we should be surprised by the similarity between us and apes – we are an ape. It might not fit comfortably with our Gucci-wearing, Porshe-driving, deodorized and sanitized image, but a visitor from space would classify us as a type of chimpanzee without hesitation. It's quite sickening when you think of the barbarity we mete out to chimpanzees in laboratories – our nearest living relatives, with whom we share over 98 per cent of our genes.

The very first primates lived some 60 million years ago and the important changes which marked our development took place then – the transition from paw to hand; the development of forward-looking eyes and overlapping visual fields, providing depth of vision and the ability to identify predators from a distance.

One of these first primates was the lemur, a vegetarian which seemed quite happy with its lot and felt no urge to stray outside its very specific forest habitat. Twenty million years later came the Anthropoids, the so-called 'higher primates', including monkeys and apes. These were much more adventurous creatures and over the next few million years they began to spread across the globe, inhabiting even quite cool areas. In their travels they ate many different types of food, which provided a richer diversity of nutrition leading to greater intelligence. They were all still vegetarian.

The outcome, about 18 million years ago, was the Hominoids, apes with larger brains, bigger bodies and no tails. One of them was Proconsul, still a vegetarian and the likely joint ancestor of the gorilla, chimpanzee and humankind, variations which came into being probably about five to six million years ago.

New research techniques can trace the genetic inheritance passed down to us through the female line. It has come up with a tiny female nicknamed Lucy as the starting-point for human evolution, three and a half million years ago. She was, in fact, one of a group called *Australopithecus afarensis* who strode across the African veldt, sheltered in the forests and waded through the waters of estuaries.

Researchers seem desperate to prove that our ancestors were rabid meat eaters almost as soon as they stood up on two legs and the discovery of another *Australopithecus* (*robustos*) had them turning cartwheels. Alongside *robustos*'s remains were discovered the bones of large mammals and the assumption was that *robustos* had eaten them. Closer investigation, however, showed that the bones had been used as tools to dig up bulbs and roots.

The first real evidence of meat eating was discovered to have begun one and a half to two million years ago – in evolutionary terms, almost yesterday – and the beings responsible were *Homo habilis*. It's thought they scavenged meat from kills made by the big cats but did not actively hunt. It's all really guesswork. However, the discovery of tools such as spearheads definitely showed that hunting started around one and a half million years ago and the guilty party was *Homo erectus*, who was around until about 200,000 years ago.

There seems to be a bizarre assumption that once they'd tasted meat, our ancestors lived on nothing else. In fact hunting was often a male social event – the primitive equivalent of going to the pub – and not that successful. The bulk of the diet was what it had always been, the produce of wild plants, some of it dried and stored. The women and children gathered the fruits, herbs, nuts, seeds and berries. These plant foods have always been the staff of life. In fact, we developed to almost the creatures we are on an entirely vegan diet and even after we began to eat meat, it constituted only a minuscule part of our diet.

There have been claims that without meat we couldn't have developed our cerebral cortex, the site of intellect and reasoning. The neutral fatty acids Omega Three and Omega Six are apparently the vital ingredients in its development and Omega

Six is found in meat. What has been overlooked is the presence of Omega Six fatty acids in over 200 plants. Omega Three is also found in some plants, nuts and seeds, but particularly in sea creatures and plants. It is where the seas meet the land, in the estuaries of great rivers with their abundance of sea-weeds and other vegetation, that development of the brain almost certainly took place. So there was no need to eat either meat or fish.

As *Homo sapiens* spread across the world, grabbing their chances opportunistically, meat obviously did become part of the diet. Hunting was invented when climactic changes destroyed the food sources in the northern regions in the great Ice Ages. But in evolutionary terms this is a very short period ago and our bodies are still vegetarian. In fact, until well into the twentieth century, meat was largely the prerogative of the rich and powerful, the peasantry only eating it at a few religious festivals, perhaps three or four times a year. But as the rich ate meat, it became associated with wealth and nearly everyone else eventually copied them. The ethos of the ruling élite will always become that of society in general.

But now, when we have aped our 'betters' so well that we are drowning in a sea of cheap animal flesh, our bodies still haven't evolved to cope with it. As a result, as already discussed, diseases such as cancer and heart disease are prospering. Meat is so unnatural to us that we usually can't even eat it without first cooking it. In fact the thought of eating a lamb or calf raw, ripping into its heart, flesh and stomach, is revolting to most people – hardly the sign of a carnivore.

Omnivores and carnivores, on the other hand, have powerful stomach acids to digest meat. Their gut is extremely short, expelling the waste products of meat, the toxins and carcinogens, as quickly as possible. The human gut, an ape's gut, is the opposite. It is extremely long and handles large amounts of fibrous material, which trundles slowly through the bowel, allowing the maximum goodness to be extracted from it.

Other illuminating differences include: carnivores have no manual dexterity, we do; carnivores pant to cool their bodies, we sweat; carnivores lap water, we sip it; and carnivores can manufacture vitamin C internally, we cannot.

Colin Spencer has written an amazingly detailed book on the history of vegetarianism called *The Heretic's Feast* (Fourth Estate, London 1994) which greatly expands on all the information here. But nothing sums up our relationship with another species more succinctly than a simple slide show. Dr David Ryde, a vegan doctor who was an adviser to the medical sub-committee of the British Olympic Association for 15 years, has carried out an interesting little test over the past decade. He showed slides of a human's and gorilla's digestive tracts and asked medical colleagues at various lectures if they could identify anything specific about them. They made different comments about whether they were male or female, but not one has ever identified one of them as being the organs of an ape.

If we eat nothing but meat and dairy products, we die. If we eat nothing but a vegan diet, not only do we stay alive but we grow and become healthier, live longer and prosper. Surely that must tell us something?

13 ◆ DEVELOPED TO DEATH

It's amazing how easy it is to become blasé. My first visit to
Majorca, when I was 18, was a magical mystery tour of foreign
lands and foods, an unintelligible language and extraordinary
blue seas and golden sands. It didn't take many years before all
European countries melded into an homogeneous blend of
similar architecture, identical advertisements and international
food. It wasn't until I went to Kenya in 1993 that I again relived
that feeling of being abroad.

The coach from the airport to my hotel went through
Mombasa and I could almost feel my jaw sagging as, dazed
with the time difference, I perspired in a baking winter sun,
breathed in new aromas, some of them on the demanding side,
and watched the throngs of people going about their day. This
was abroad, this was the developing world, this was chaos.
The 1930s art deco shop fronts, rusting corrugated iron roofs,
jostling black and Indian traders; the car horns, moped engines,
bicycle bells and the clamour of human voices selling and
buying and shouting; the awareness that this was normality
and I was the visitor, I was the foreigner.

This was the continent that the British, Germans, Belgians,
French, Italians, Dutch and Portuguese divided up between
themselves in the eighteenth and nineteenth centuries in order

to share out the rich pickings. Ruler lines were drawn through large swathes of territory, through the middle of tribal lands and customs and languages – French to the left, British to the right, a wealth of culture and history, knowledge and understanding reduced to the level of commodity suppliers.

The colonists arrived and ruled, learning almost nothing from those they subjugated, integrating hardly at all. And here I was, still part of that ruling culture. The pith helmets and white knees of the infantry regiments might have gone, but the West's control is still absolute. It is now done through the United Africa Company or Lohnro or Unilever or Rio Tinto Zinc and other multinational corporations.

These multinationals, which have grown up in the latter half of the twentieth century, know no national boundaries and move production to wherever it is cheapest or most friendly in terms of anti-trade union legislation or wherever the most generous financial incentives are being offered. Many individual corporations have greater financial clout than some entire countries. They are a law unto themselves and have only one overriding concern – to show a profit for their shareholders. None of the other human, social, environmental or political considerations which might exert some influence over national companies are of any concern to them. They are heavily involved in meat production and one of their greatest influences, often encouraged by Governments hungry for hard currency with which to meet their debts, has been to take control of huge areas of land right across the world. Every new acquisition leads to more people being dispossessed and in some countries it has affected one third of all rural people. In Latin America it is more than 40 per cent.[1]

Import tariffs are another part of the West's control. For the import of cheap cash crops into Europe we charge little in the way of duties, but if African countries try to increase the value of their exports by processing them, turning them into products, raising their value, we impose heavy duties, pricing them out of the market. We preserve the right to add that value ourselves, enabling our industries to prosper. When we have done so, we often export back to the same countries the products we originally obtained from them but at inflated prices.

Also, we have encouraged the obnoxious élites who rule so many African and other ex-colonial countries, providing them with their ethos as well as the loans with which to buy their armies and their weaponry – usually from us – as insurance against revolution by their own people. Once they are established in power and saddled with debt, it is the poor of those countries who are pushed further and further into a subsistence existence by having to pay the interest off. Despite the overpowering wealth of Western countries, the net transfer of money is from the developing world to the developed world.

It is disturbing, but no other economic system is on offer anywhere in the world. From Borneo to Brazil, Somalia to Sumatra, profit is now the global penicillin. And this philosophy which has created a world of haves and have nots claims to be the only one which can eliminate those divisions. It is tantamount to a seventeenth-century quack physician prescribing bleeding for a patient dying from a haemorrhage.

And of course it is a lie. Our leaders care little how many children die from starvation or how impoverished are their parents. When more than one million children die from measles every year for the want of a 9p vaccine – total cost less than one year's pay increase for the chairman of British Gas – it puts things into some kind of perspective.

The world's problems are discussed by suited men whose vocabulary is lacking such words as 'vision' and 'compassion', 'care' and 'concern', 'honesty' and 'trust'. All the great concepts which have exercised philosophers through the ages have been reduced to profit and loss. We have set the greatest store by the things of least value. And with all the monumental challenges of the world to face, our leaders can think no further than the next election. So they continue to exploit anything which might provide some short-term advantage – humans, other animals, the world's resources. They have the resources and knowledge to end hunger throughout the world, but reduce their aid budget. They ensure that the gulf between rich and poor widens at home, profess concern for the raging poverty abroad and do nothing about either. There is no longer any dialogue about development issues, only excuses and clichés and cynicism.

All these thoughts were no longer abstract in my mind as the coach headed beneath the metal, elephant-tusk arch over the only dual carriageway in Mombasa, out of the city and its bustle and along the bush-fringed road towards Malindi. The hotel was on the coast some 20 kilometres from the city, although it was in itself a mini conurbation. Small blocks were distributed throughout the most wonderfully colourful grounds, dripping with bougainvillaea, shaded by coconut palms and tended by deferential hotel staff. It was, of course, fenced off from the rest of the world and patrolled by tall, black, silent, robed security men who looked like extras from the film *King Solomon's Mines*.

Outside the fence was a complete mini-shanty town from which the labourers to run the hotel were drawn. They lived two families to a two-room shack with mud walls, papered with the pictures cut from old newspapers. Worldly possessions amounted to part-share of a small cardboard suitcase beneath a settle bed.

These and the people like them, we are told, are the cause of the world's great problems with their non-stop production of children. These criticisms, of course, conveniently ignore reality. A child of the United States will, in its lifetime, consume 12 times as much of the world's resources as the children born to these Kikuyu tribespeople, huddled beneath the perimeter fence of a posh hotel – 12 times as much oil, copper, zinc, water, steel and, most importantly, land.[2]

In a world of profligacy, these people's struggle for survival is made worse by tourism. The demands of new hotels, which stretch along the coast from both sides of Mombasa, distort local food prices, driving them upwards and placing some produce out of the hands of the poorest.

You could, however, feel the sense of community and sharing there. They cooked communally, their food almost entirely free from meat, and after their evening meal they sat together, talking, laughing and listening to the BBC World Service. Crying babies were passed from hand to hand until soothed and satisfied. And they talked proudly of their beautiful, colourful country beneath the flaming scarlet blossoms of a flamboya tree.

Meantime, inside the hotel, Europeans smeared themselves with sun tan oil, ate European food, drank European drinks and spoke infrequently to each other. At lunch and dinner they were carved thick slices of meat from huge roast joints or helped themselves to pieces from enormous baked fish. The clash of cultures was so extreme that it could have been Martians and Venusians on an intergalactic weekend break.

While the carvery was offering an inexhaustible supply of cooked dead animals to a select few, much of the world's population was starving. This is a phenomenon which stretches across Africa, Asia and South America, all continents which have been invaded and colonized.

Through the eyes of a visiting European, the problem looks exactly as we have been taught – too many poor people struggling against an inhospitable land and climate and producing too many children as a form of insurance. That is only partly true. People with a history older than our own and with a rich and vibrant culture could not have spent that entire history struggling on the margins for survival. And, of course, they didn't. Many things have played a part in the impoverishment of great tracts of the world and high amongst them is the West's addiction to meat and animal protein. The little vignette of the carvery and its overloaded plates inside the hotel and the meagre dishes of maize and rice outside lies at the root of many of the world's seemingly most intractable problems.

When the early explorers of the sixteenth and seventeenth centuries landed in Africa they didn't find starvation, but an abundance of food. Everyone lived from the land and it was common for people to have two or three harvests preserved or stored away. The whole concept of buying and selling food did not exist.

The needs of our industrial revolution were for plentiful and cheap raw materials and for those we scoured the world. When we found them, not only did we take them away but also sovereignty and independence, dispossessing unsophisticated people of their land and then charging them rent for what had once been theirs by right. In order to meet the demands of their landlords, these new tenants were obliged to grow the crops which their masters valued – cotton, hemp, cocoa – and it was the masters who determined the price they would pay.

You don't even need to go as far as Africa to witness the effects of colonization, a simple trip across the Irish Sea will do. The expropriation of land from poor farmers and its gift to the landed gentry led to the depopulation of Ireland. When blight destroyed the potato crop in the 1840s and country people could not pay their rents, they were simply evicted from their homes and the homes destroyed. One million died and two million emigrated, while England imported twice as much food from Ireland as would have been needed to feed the entire population of that country.

It was the same all over the world. The colonists took a system which worked well for Africa or Asia, destroyed it and substituted a system which worked for Europe. It set indigenous people on a cycle of debt and dependency which was enforced by the élites of their own kind, who were courted and flattered and shaped in the image of the colonists. Once the countries became independent, these élites continued that exploitative enforcement.

The first section of the road from Mombasa to Malindi is flanked on either side by woods and bushland, with occasional villages surrounded by small vegetable patches and coconut palms. This homogeny ends dramatically, giving way to kilo-metre upon kilometre of sisal, neatly planted rows of vegetation which are not for local use but for export. How many villages were uprooted, how many people dispossessed, how many vegetable plots ploughed under to provide the land?

This kind of scheme is frequently enforced by the World Bank or International Monetary Fund as part of 'debt restruc-turing' or to qualify for 'development loans'. But it is still the West calling the tune and the rest of the world dancing to it. And part of that control is to ensure that plentiful and cheap cattle fodder is available to satisfy our enormous appetite for meat.

A set of simple statistics provides a perspective. One fifth of the world's population lives in extreme poverty and one third of the world's entire population of children is malnourished.[3] Over 12 million of them die every year from poverty and hunger-related diseases.[4] Meanwhile, one quarter of the world's fish catch is fed to animals,[5] as is one third of the grain production.[6] In the US and EC, the figures are more startling – almost three quarters of their grain is fed to livestock.[7] It is now necessary to scour the world in search of feed for the swelling numbers of livestock – and with the human population expected to increase by almost 20 per cent in the next decade, the makings of a world-wide food crisis are already in the offing.

In Britain, in 1946, approximately two million cattle, 7.4 million sheep, 2.2 million pigs and about 40 million chickens were slaughtered.[8] In 1994 numbers had increased to 3.2 million cattle, 19 million sheep, 15 million pigs and 676 million chickens.[9] This growth is reflected across the whole of the developed world, each country swelling its meat production in an orgy of consumption which, in many cases, has led to animal protein being consumed at virtually every meal. There have not been corresponding increases in the human population; in fact these have been extremely small in most countries.

There is not enough grass for the huge numbers involved and the speed at which animals grow on this natural diet is too slow for the profit-hungry producers. So it is substituted by grain, oil seeds, soya, fish meal and often the ground-up remains of animals, including their own kind.

In fact, 60 per cent of EC animal feeds[10] and 90 per cent of the protein concentrates used for animal feed in Britain[11] are imported from the developing world – the same countries whose children are dying for want of protein – and much of that animal fodder is ideal for human consumption. It has been estimated that the amount of food required to eliminate the most extreme cases of hunger around the world is about 40 million tonnes. The amount of grain which developed countries feed to animals is some 540 million tonnes.[12]

The answer to all these problems, we are told, is the market philosophy, whereas it is, in fact, the cause. The same grains can be used to feed either animals or humans, but they are not distributed on the basis of need or the promptings of conscience but sold to the highest bidder. The highest bidder is

invariably the wealthy, the livestock owners, the possessors
of capital.

Most grain is produced in the West and some of it is
exported to the developing world, but the trade gap in food is
all in our favour. We import 40 per cent more high-quality
protein from the developing world than we export to it.[13] Two
of these foods – peanuts and soya – are imported into Europe
because that is cheaper than buying animal feed which is grown
here. India alone, with some of the greatest health and malnutrition problems in the world, has increased its exports of soya
beans five-fold between 1974 and 1982.[14]

This phenomenon is exacerbated by the growing inequali-
ties in wealth. The fewer people who can afford to buy the food
grown in their home countries, the greater the incentive for
their own Governments and landowners to grow cash crops for
export instead, particularly animal fodder as the demand seems
inexhaustible.

Of all the Western appetites, the United States has the most
voracious. It is responsible for 75 per cent of the entire global
production of soya beans.[15] Every vegetarian and vegan knows
the extraordinary value of soya beans and the huge variety of
high-protein, low-fat foods which can be made from them.
Despite this, the US feeds almost its entire crop to animals in
the most inefficient, wasteful and damaging addiction the
world has ever seen.[16]

According to Professor Colin Spedding of the University
of Reading's Agriculture Department, a Western meat-based
diet uses four and a half times more land than is necessary for a
vegan diet and two and a quarter more than for a vegetarian
diet.[17] An analogy commonly quoted is this: imagine an area of
land the size of five football pitches (10 hectares). It will grow
enough meat to feed two people; or maize to feed 10; or grain to
feed 24; or soya to feed 61. There is more than enough arable

land to feed the present world human population on a vegan diet, but nowhere near enough for the animal produce centred American one.[18]

For every 10 kilograms of soya protein fed to America's cattle only one kilogram is converted into meat, the remainder being excreted. Almost the entire population of India and China, nearly two billion people, could be fed on the protein consumed and largely wasted by the United States' beef herd.

When you take a global perspective, the problem assumes such proportions that it is hard to comprehend. So much land in the poorer, developing countries has been turned over to growing feed for livestock that it now amounts to 14.6 million hectares – and that is solely to supply the EC.[19] If that figure leaves you cold, then try visualizing the amount of productive land – not mountains or swamps or deserts or jungles, but crop land – that would make up the entire area of the United Kingdom. Add to that France, some four times our size, then Italy and New Zealand and you have some idea of the area. That in itself is a big enough problem, but compound it with the complete lack of independence of those who produce the fodder and you have the potential to turn disaster into catastrophe.

There are worrying portents for the future. After 40 years of steady expansion, the world's grain harvest began to fall in the late 1980s. From a position where stocks amounted to 459 million tonnes, enough to feed the entire world for 101 days, stocks have reduced to 240 million tonnes, only enough to last 54 days.[20]

Part of the problem is the reduction in soil fertility after so many years of monoculture supported by saturating the soil with chemical fertilizers, pesticides and herbicides. As grain stocks reduce, if there is not a change in philosophy, cattle will further take precedence over people and the downward spiral of starvation and poverty will be given another vicious twist.

Not satisfied with imposing its greed and economic system on the world, the West is now increasing the demand for animal fodder by exporting the abhorrent factory-farming systems which were responsible for the explosion of meat eating in the West. Throughout the Indian sub-continent, battery hen systems and broiler houses have become widespread. Employing almost no people and consuming valuable protein, these systems don't even begin to address the needs of the population, the majority of whom can't afford to buy the eggs and meat. But that was never the intention. Apart from satisfying its own middle classes, much of the produce is exported to the Gulf States, providing even more and cheaper animal protein to countries already saturated with choice.

People are not starving because of a shortage of food – there is more than enough for everyone. The problem is one of use and distribution. The incredible inefficiency of animals in converting vegetable protein into animal protein – a ratio which can be as high as 16:1 – is obviously one of the most significant factors at work. It is encouraged by the all-pervasive concept that West is best. Quite naturally, people who are impoverished look at our affluence and think they would like some of what we have. And we encourage the rest of the world to emulate our habits, practices and tastes – including eating meat. For them it is a totally unachievable aspiration.

The present population of the world is about 5,600 billion people. On a plant-food diet every single person could receive the 2,360 Kcal (calories) daily necessary to live a healthy life. In fact, even with the amount of food currently grown, another 600 million people could be fed on a vegan diet. However, if 35 per cent of those calories are supplied by animal protein, the world can support only 2,500 billion people.[21]

In simple, brutal terms, the world can feed less than half its present population using a typical US, meat-based diet. With the population expected to grow by 90 million a year for the next 40 years,[22] the prospects are dismal.

The problem of overconsumption is a problem of the West, while the problem of overpopulation is a problem of the developing world – and the two are intimately linked. The cure for overpopulation is security, sufficient food, stability, access to health care and the possibility of fulfilling aspirations, all of which remove the need for 'insurance' births. Meantime, however, exploitation continues.

I visited Thailand in 1994 and its capital city, Bangkok, is a monument to the 'thrusting', 'dynamic', 'successful' economies of the Pacific Rim. On the other hand you could call it a concrete jungle with the worst traffic problems in the world – a monument to capitalism unhindered by the costs of little things like health services, secondary education or even fundamental welfare.

One of the most shaming and highly visible failures of this philosophy is the seemingly endless supply of teenage prostitutes of both sexes. They are on display in the bars and clubs of Pat Pong and Sukhumvit and at the tourist resorts of Patia and Phuket, while almost every newspaper and magazine is filled with not-so-discreetly worded advertisements for their services. They arrive most days at the huge and crowded Hualumpong station, nearly all on trains from the north.

Along the road beside the station are the offices of numerous agents who sign up young people with promises of wealth and then sell them into virtual slavery in backroom factories. The sex industry recruiters are more subtle, usually having struck deals with the children's parents before they have even left home.

I spoke to some of these very young people, most of them

high or slurring on drugs or drink. Their stories were all individual but had common threads running through them. They were all the sons and daughters of northern rural families who had become impoverished through loss of land, failing water supplies or low prices. Typical was the great tapioca fiasco.

Over the 10 years to 1985, thousands of square kilometres of rainforest were cleared in order to grow tapioca for the EC's livestock. When beef and pork production levelled off and mountains of unused meat began to grow, the EC simply stopped buying Thai tapioca. People who had impoverished themselves to buy farming equipment to help them meet the demand suddenly found themselves without an income. I was assured that some were so poor that they would scrape slime from the bottom of ponds and eat it because of the nutrients it contained.

Meantime in Haiti, officially designated as one of the world's poorest countries, much of the best agricultural land is used for growing alfalfa. In an act of complete obscenity, multinational beef concerns fly cattle from Texas to Haiti to graze and fatten on the alfalfa before flying them back to Texas as carcasses for US hamburgers.

Poor, dispossessed Haitians have been pushed on to the mountain slopes where they try to live by farming the poorest soil on the island. The result is overgrazing, soil depletion and a drop in soil fertility leading to environmental degradation. A disaster from whatever perspective, it is one which is being repeated all over the world. Increasingly, the poorest two thirds of the planet is sliding inexorably deeper into a life of starvation and poverty in order to support the wealthiest one third.

So our much-vaunted lifestyle based around 'choice' is not choice at all, because the true effects are hidden from us and choice without information is valueless. In reality it is the right of large companies and national Governments to prosper on the backs of starving and increasingly impoverished people – and to threaten the existence of the planet in the process.

Prior to its Sandinista revolution, Nicaragua was the leading Latin American supplier of beef to the US but it also had huge social problems which remained largely ignored by its right-wing dictatorship. The condition on which the US extended aid to Nicaragua had nothing to do with helping the poor but everything to do with increasing beef supplies. As a consequence, 1,000 kilometres of rainforest was destroyed annually to provide grazing for cattle.

Similarly in Costa Rica, another big supplier of beef to the US, hamburgers took precedence over the preservation of vital forest. The World Bank, which holds the ultimate levers to world finance, would only advance loans in the 1970s on condition that rainforest was cleared, again to supply beef to a section of the world which is drowning in a surfeit of the stuff.

Between 1971 and 1977, over $3.5 billion in loans[23] and technical assistance poured into Latin America for cattle farming. This is part of a systematic effort by multinational corporations to control the world's industries for the benefit of developed nations at the expense of the poor. These loans have been responsible for dispossessing the powerless and catastrophic environmental damage. Countries like Mexico are hardest hit by this newest form of neocolonial exploitation, as more and more land is converted to grassland for cattle. Mexico ships much of its cattle to the USA, where it is killed for meat.[24]

In Brazil, 23 per cent of agricultural land is currently used to grow soya beans, of which half are for export.[25] This has resulted in less food for the native people as staple foods become increasingly expensive, as farmers switch to growing soya for the more lucrative international animal feed market.[26]

The latest batch of statistics from the World Health Organization, in its report entitled *Bridging the Gaps* (1995), reveals that the shaming problem of impoverishment is getting worse:

> Poverty wields its destructive influence at every stage of human life, from the moment of conception to the grave. It conspires with the most deadly and painful diseases to bring a wretched existence to all who suffer from it.[27]

The report shows a gulf developing between rich and poor, north and south, men and women, employed and unemployed, young and old. It even identifies the same problem in the wealthy, developed nations, where the poorest, most disadvantaged groups are falling further and further behind:

> The unemployed are a potent reminder of the dangers of assuming that the general prosperity of a country will trickle down to all its members.[28]

And:

> There has been a disproportionate flow of resources from the developing to the developed world – poor countries paying money to rich ones – because of debt servicing and repayment and as a consequence of prices for raw materials that favour the latter at the expense of the former. Structural adjustment policies [that is, IMF and World Bank loan conditions] aimed at improving the economic performance of poor countries have, in many cases, made the situation worse.[29]

What the report is describing is a global catastrophe.

A similar damning report was produced in the late 1970s by the Brandt Commission, headed by the ex-German Chancellor Willie Brandt.[30] Ex-British Prime Minister Edward Heath was also on the commission. The conclusions were that unless there was a dramatic change in the attitude of the wealthy countries of the world towards the poorer, and a major shift of resources, there would be famine, bloodshed and catastrophe on a scale never before seen in history.

It was ignored, just as this latest report will be ignored. Governments will not change their policies because to do so would threaten the control and resources which maintain them in power. Fortunately, we, as individuals, *can* do something.

Meat consumption is obviously not the only reason for world hunger, but it is high up there in the major league. It is also something which we don't need permission to do something about. We can wield an immediate influence today, simply by changing our diet. By not eating meat or fish, vegetarians reduce the need to import food from poor countries, but a vegetarian diet does more than that. It throws down a challenge to the established order and breaks the cycle whereby people go hungry while ever-increasing numbers of appallingly treated animals are fed huge amounts of food in a hopelessly inefficient system.

Vegetarians, and even more so vegans, use far fewer of the world's resources of food, land and energy, and offer the only feasible example for the future. Unless there is a positive global move towards this way of living, the expanding world population will be condemned to disease and suffering on an unimaginable scale. In a desperate search for protein, all the living creatures on the globe will be hunted and killed. The wonderful diversity of living things, the last of a species, the most beautiful of creations, will mean nothing more than a mouthful of food to get a family through another day. And we will wring our hands and ask how on Earth it happened.

14 ◆ A MATTER OF ENVIRONMENT

One reason for going to Kenya was to clarify my mind about the future. Despite my position as Director of the Vegetarian Society, decisions were being taken by the governing council which I found disturbing. Two very distinct views on the direction in which we should be heading had developed, with the majority of the staff on one side and the council on the other. All the values I believed in were, it seemed to me, being jettisoned in a stampede to commercialize the organization. The council was dancing with the Devil, not to try and change him, but to learn from him. I had to decide what I wanted to do.

Another reason for going was to fulfil a lifelong ambition and see wild animals on the plains of Africa. The trek from Mombasa to the Amboseli Game Reserve is a tortuous and dusty one – and uncomfortable as the minibus lurches, sways and bumps over kilometres of dirt track and eventually crosses a black and desolate lava flow many kilometres wide. This is the point at which vehicles draw together in convoy for self-protection. Not from animals but from humans.

This is poacher territory and the same people who are prepared to kill an elephant for its ivory are equally prepared to rob tourists. A rhino had been killed the previous week so that its horn could be sold to the Yemen for use by some wealthy oil producer as a dagger handle. On this occasion, fortunately, the poachers didn't reveal themselves to us.

The first large animal I saw was one of the most bizarre sights I have ever witnessed. Years of TV documentaries had not prepared me for it. We were miles from Amboseli in open land, a mixture of scrub, trees and grazing for Masai cattle. A giraffe, unconcerned and uninterested, stepped out of the trees, loping as though it had just learnt to walk. It looked huge and incongruous, like an enormous bendy-toy, and its gaudy ginger mottled colouring offered no camouflage but seemed to shout: 'Here I am!' It had the look of something born of Walt Disney's imagination rather than a product of evolution. Behind it, the towering, conical peak of Mount Kilimanjaro poked its summit through a ring of clouds, like the bald head of a monk showing through the halo of his hair. The creature looked completely vulnerable and totally unfitted to an age of motor vehicles and rifles. It is an image which will stay with me.

Eventually we arrived at the reserve and after checking into the sheer luxury of a safari lodge, I began my first 'game drive'. The minibus came to a halt on the edge of a dusty track surrounded by open plains but the driver kept the engine running. On three sides, as far as the eye could see, there was nothing but scrubby grassland. Kilimanjaro occupied the fourth side. Swirls of warm wind raised small clouds of dust. Occasionally they spiralled into dust devils, tiny tornadoes which twisted and turned hundreds of metres up into the air. The animals ignored the dust devils, ignored us and appeared to ignore each other as they grazed on the sparse pastures.

Over to the left, a huge herd of elephants stood almost motionless, so far away that they looked like little models. To the right, a lone matriarch with a solitary tusk came towards us, heading home to her herd. She may have been off seeking new pastures or perhaps just visiting relatives. This huge, grey, prehistoric creature, which lives by all the codes we associate with greatness – care, concern, understanding, patience, compassion and love – continued towards us, her pace unrelenting. With her huge bulk, her great curving tusk and her small eyes, which seemed to look nowhere but ahead, towards her family, she plodded on with remorseless weariness, just as her ancestors have done for millions of years. I wanted to cry.

As this glorious creature receded into the distance I looked around me. I was surrounded by buffalo and antelope, gnu and zebra, wart hogs and giraffe. The beauty and diversity of this incredible planet almost took my breath away. But when white men first discovered the continent of Africa, they weren't humbled by what they saw. They barely wrote of its beauty; they didn't contemplate their minuscule part in all this majesty as some other great civilizations have done. No, they took guns and killed as many creatures as they could and called it sport. They made umbrella stands from elephants' feet, carved useless trinkets from their tusks, made ashtrays from the hands of gorillas, stuffed heads and placed them on their walls to stare forever in glassy-eyed immobility. The people of Africa, who for centuries had mostly lived in harmony with the other animals, they enslaved.

Back on the game reserve I glimpsed the head of a cheetah in some patchy grass, 200 metres away. Suddenly, she sat up, alert, intent, her eyes fixed on … something. In an unhurried, ambling walk she came towards us, her head stretched forward, her long, lean body tensed. As she drew level, the walk became a trot and she passed us by, not even glancing in our direction.

Like a coiled spring being released, the trot then was transformed into an electrifying burst of speed and within seconds the cheetah was almost out of clear sight, a dusty trail marking her devastating progress. Two other dusty trails – a mother Thomson's gazelle and its young – started up ahead of her and almost matched her for speed – almost. After a short and frantic chase, one trail veered off to the right and the other continued straight ahead. It was this one the cheetah followed. There was a tumbling, cartwheeling cloud of dust as the kill was made. Within seconds the plain had returned to its timeless calm.

The cheetah has evolved to live almost exclusively on meat and in particular on Thomson's gazelles. The Tommies who are weak, unwell or not sufficiently agile don't survive into adulthood to pass their inferior genes on to their offspring. There is a bond between the two, between the hunted and the hunter. It is a bond of dependence. Without it, neither would be the creature it is. It is a bond based on need, not on cruelty.

People think they're being terribly clever when they say to vegetarians: 'Well, animals eat each other, so why shouldn't we?' Some animals live in holes in the ground or sleep in trees or stick their noses up each other's bottoms as a form of introduction but fortunately we don't choose to do any of these things. Yes, some animals do eat other animals, but they have no choice and when they do dispense death they mostly do it quickly.

The African plains were wonderful but a dispiriting feeling grew in me during my time there. It was the awareness that game parks such as Amboseli, Savo and Shimba Hills are fast becoming the last resort for Africa's wildlife. The animals now live on our terms, on land defined by us, under the constant gaze of human eyes in the dozens of safari buses which daily chase around the parks. It is impossible to avoid the conclusion that the animals' tenancy is likely to be a short one. I had the distinct feeling that almost anything could threaten the existence of the parks, but particularly the burgeoning human population. People will not stand forever outside the perimeters, landless and hungry.

Even as I was writing this chapter, news came through that

the Ngorogoro crater, one of Africa's most unique game parks, is being put up for sale to Western buyers in order to raise hard currency. Africa's animals have become a commodity to be traded on the international markets!

The pressure is coming from all sides. The animals which depend upon migration are having their migration routes closed off by farmers. Any creature which strays outside the artificial boundaries created by humans is likely to be shot, not because it is dangerous but because it eats grass and shrubs.

The poacher's rifle, snare or poison dart spells death for some – the elephant and the rhino – but the hump-backed, curving-horned, doe-eyed, domesticated cattle of the Africa plains could eventually spell the death of most wildlife. All around Amboseli, the Masai Mara and other Kenyan game parks, the elegant, red-robed Masai tribespeople, with their plaited hair and painted faces, tend huge herds of cows. For centuries, when the cows they reared were only for their own use, they largely lived in harmony with nature. But now that cow meat is a commodity that can be sold to the wealthy and the white (the majority of Africans can't afford it), the number of animals has increased dramatically. Alongside them have grown the herds owned by wealthy ranchers and multinational corporations. As the number of cattle increases, so do all the problems they bring with them.

Many of the people who go on safari do so because of their love of and concern for wildlife. They take pictures, buy T-shirts and contribute to funds to save endangered species. But when they arrive at the safari lodge in the evening, they eat their beef or pork or chicken and fail to make the connection. By eating meat they are killing the wildlife as surely as if they shot it with a rifle. The only difference is that the method of death meat eaters bring to wildlife is more permanent, more certain and more difficult to reverse, because once the habitat is gone there is little chance of a return.

Of course the single biggest loss of habitat is the destruction of the rainforests. They say there is only one human-made structure which can be identified from space and that is the Great Wall of China. But there is a human-made catastrophe which astronauts could see quite clearly in 1989. It was the billowing clouds of smoke which stretched across thousands of kilometres of South America as large sections of Amazonia were put to the torch in a never-ending orgy of destruction.

It isn't a new phenomenon. For a couple of centuries or more we have used timber from the forests of the world. Britain itself was once largely forest and almost the entire landscape that we can now see was made by human hand. We have reduced our forest cover from over 80 per cent to a mere 1.5 per cent – over half has been destroyed in the last 50 years.[1] And we're still cutting. As late as 1950, about 14 per cent of the world's surface was cloaked in tropical forest. It is now down to less than 7 per cent.[2]

People talk about tropical rainforests with concern but they are still something outside the experience of most of us and as such it can be hard to feel personally involved with their destruction. I've always wanted to see them for myself – partly because I feel certain that they will not be here for that much longer.

In perhaps not the best decision of my life, I chose to go to Belize in Central America, to the forests of what was British Honduras, for my honeymoon. Sleeping in jungle camps, in dormitories and communal shacks, rising at 5.30 a.m., bumping along dirt tracks with a driver dressed in a sea captain's uniform, serenading you with his own karaoke, is not the stuff of romance. But there were compensations: washing away the sweat by swimming in a chilled, deep pool beneath a forest waterfall; watching the energetic dash of scarlet macaws as they squawk to each other in tuneless enthusiasm; diving into the deep green waters of a river with nothing but trees as the backdrop; listening to the boom of a howler monkey – and dodging the sticks thrown by it.

The forests of Central America are, like all rainforests, nature in perfect balance. When the rain falls, it falls in stair-rods with a hissing, roaring intensity, the spray from the droplets forming a low-level mist. The forests help cause the rain and the rain sustains the forests. The soil in which the trees stand is unusually thin, but their roots and the leaf litter on the forest floor hold the rain, quickly absorbing it and using it to carry nutrients up through the trunk to the leaves which form the canopy before it evaporates back into the atmosphere as water vapour. Those same leaves, when they fall and rot and join the other litter on the forest floor, provide that essential food on which the forest prospers.

These trees are the lungs of the planet. They draw carbon dioxide (CO_2) from the atmosphere and lock it into their structure, while new growth releases life-giving oxygen in return. When the CO_2 is finally released it is only slowly, when the trees eventually die and decompose.

The forest grows at three levels – the shrubs, bushes and new palms at head height; full grown palms at mid-height; and then, towering over everything, the huge mahogany and other hardwood trees. Sunlight dapples through the foliage and although there is a sense of life teeming all around there are few signs of it. Yet turn over a stone and beneath it might be a tiny but deadly pink coral snake; look carefully and, immobile on the end of a branch, you might see the forest dragon, the prehistoric and entirely harmless iguana; or listen carefully as the sun rises and you might, if you're lucky, hear the deep-throated purr of a jaguar, content with its night-time kill.

No one knows how many different plants and animals constitute the flora and fauna of the forests because there are still innumerable discoveries to be made, but it is estimated that at least one half of all the world's species lives here.[3] Tropical forests are the main dispensary of raw materials for modern medicines – antibiotics, heart drugs, tranquillizers, ulcer treatments, hormones and many others. Seventy per cent of the plants identified as having anti-cancer properties are from the rainforests.[4] Thanks to the rosy periwinkle, a child suffering from leukaemia now has an 80 per cent chance of survival instead of 20 per cent.[5]

And what do we do with these extraordinarily vibrant ecosystems? We chop them down to create grazing for cattle, which will largely be exported to the developed world as frozen beef and hamburger meat. The process known as 'slash and burn' eradicates all growth in bonfires of insanity, unlocking centuries' worth of stored CO_2 in only minutes, permitting it to drift upwards into the stratosphere and spread around the world in a mantle which traps its radiated heat – global warming!

As for the people who live in the forests, they are pushed deeper into the parts which remain, are shot, dispossessed and left to die of alcoholism or diseases to which they have no resistance. They are introduced to such developed and 'civilized' pursuits as prostitution, enslavement and begging.

The thin and infertile grassland which replaces the forest is largely handed over to multinational corporations or supporters of the ruling élites, who use it to grow soya beans to feed to cattle or to graze cattle directly – not for the starving of their own country but to sell in order to enrich themselves. The figures from Guatemala show the truth of this statement. Seventy-five per cent of the children under five years old are malnourished, yet every year its ranchers export 20 million kilograms of beef to the US.[6]

Reports from countries throughout Central and South America are equally depressing, as is the influence of the United States on their trade and agricultural policies. Since 1950, two thirds of lowland tropical forest in Central America have been cleared for cattle ranching. Most of the beef is exported, 80 to 90 per cent going to North America.[7] Because the meat is too lean for American tastes, it is mainly used to make hamburgers for sale by fast food chains.[8] Here, too, the cattle trade has not helped the poor. In Costa Rica, per capita beef consumption fell by more than 40 per cent between 1960 and 1979, while production rose 3.5 times.[9]

Costa Rica was once almost entirely clad in forest and this tiny land area is estimated to have held 5 per cent of the world's entire animal and plant species.[10] After a 20-year period of rapacious beef production, some of it insisted upon by the World Bank, only 17 per cent of the forests remain – and they are still being felled. Just one hamburger made from Costa Rican beef is estimated to cost the life of a large tree, 50 saplings and seedlings of some 20 to 30 different species, hundreds of species of insects and a huge diversity of mosses, fungi and micro-organisms.[11] It's only an educated guess, but it is thought that upwards of 1,000 species of all kinds become extinct every year and most of these are – or rather were – part of the rainforests.

The unwitting cattle who graze this denuded land add a further twist to the spiral of environmental damage by belching out and farting some 200 litres of methane each, every day, from their ruminant digestive processes.[12] Methane is 20 times more effective at warming the globe than CO_2,[13] which it joins above the Earth. Between them, belching and biomass burning make the second largest contribution to global warming after fossil fuel burning. Even the cleared land adds further to the problem with the release of nitrous oxide from fertilizers, one of the most potent warming agents and 150 times more damaging than CO_2.[14]

Perhaps one of the greatest 'successes' of the environmental polluters and the Governments which represent them has been their trivialization of the environmental changes taking place. In order to avoid taking any action, they have belittled the science behind the warning predictions and presented global warming as a bit of a jolly thing, really. People in northern countries will get a Mediterranean climate and be able to grow peaches. There might be a few tempests and storms and Mauritius might disappear, but on the whole, not too much to worry about!

What they omit to tell us is that no one knows the real impact it will have. We do know that large areas of the globe will be flooded as the ice caps melt and the oceans warm and expand. This will include some of the most productive land and countries and cities with multi-million populations, such as Bangkok, Egypt and Bangladesh,[15] leading to mass migrations of landless people and no spare land on which to support them. Britain and Ireland will not escape – Bill Carter of the Department of Environmental Studies, University of Ulster, identifies 25 places at risk, including Aberdeen, Dublin, the coastlines of Essex, north Kent and Lincolnshire.[16]

The most chilling scenario of them all is the impact of warming on the tundra regions of the world. These lands contain within their frozen soil an incalculable amount of methane. As the soil defrosts, billions of tonnes of the gas may be released to add to and increase global warming. The more the Earth warms, the more methane will be released in an uncontrollable, unstoppable phenomenon known as positive feedback.[17] Where it might end not even the forecasters dare predict.

The cattle are the innocent party in all this, but nevertheless their destructive influence is wider than just their flatulence. Their comparatively huge weight can cause soil to be compacted by their hooves, eventually destroying its structure. On ex-rainforest land, which is thin and unproductive to begin with, it is only a matter of a few years, seven or eight at the most, before the soil deteriorates to a point where it can no longer support grazing and is well on the way to becoming little more than a carbon copy of the great dustbowl which devastated the American West between the wars – and for similar reasons.

My own abiding memory of the tropical rainforests was a scene just outside Belize City – called a city more in hope than in any reflection of its size. Preserved from the almost total devastation which has denuded Guatemala, Nicaragua and other Central American countries, Belize still has 70 per cent of its forests, although these, its Government has decided for commercial reasons, are to be exploited until only 30 per cent remain. In fact the cleared land I was looking at was not being grazed but lingered in bepuddled, scrubby devastation. On the road in front of me was the writhing body of dying snake. It was the beautifully marked but highly venomous fer de lance and clearly visible were the tyre marks of a lorry which had purposely swerved so as to run over this normally shy and retiring reptile.

Standing motionless in the scrubland some 200 metres away was the incongruously large jabiru stork, standing over 1.5 metres tall and with a wing span of almost 3.5 metres. One of the largest birds in the world, the jabiru is probably beyond salvation, certainly in Belize, at the northern limits of its range, where only a few dozen remain. The vulnerability of both snake and stork I found acutely painful.

When I looked back towards the town I had just left, I wondered what on Earth had been gained from all the destruction.

Poverty you can smell, drunken men attempting to intimidate you into parting with a dollar or two, a desperate scramble to survive? This is the best that's on offer for many and no one pretends that continued destruction will produce anything better.

When we look at our own European or North American landscapes, we tend to assume that all the major environmental problems lie elsewhere. If only!

In Britain, for example, almost one half of all arable land is at risk of erosion – its structure has been so destroyed that wind and water can simply carry it away.[18] One of the main reasons for the breakdown is livestock production, which demands a staggering 90 per cent of all agricultural land either for grazing or fodder. Sixty to 70 per cent of the vegetable crops grown in the UK are fed to animals.[19]

The growth in the number of animals since the Second World War can only be supported by pushing the fertility of the soil to the limits – and increasingly beyond. It is done with such an array of chemicals – some 2,000 or more – that it is perhaps not surprising that some of the biggest and most successful multinational companies are now the pharmaceutical corporations. The onslaught is essentially twofold: nitrogen-based fertilizers and chemical pesticides. The old concept of rotation, growing different types of crop over a four-year period, including one year in which the land is left fallow, has largely been usurped by chemicals. Every year, a billion gallons of pesticide spray lands on British crops. Around 50 of the 200 used are strongly suspected of causing cancer. More promote allergies, birth defects and other health problems.[20]

Look carefully at almost any part of the country, but particularly East Anglia, the Midlands and South Downs, and you will see the same crops grown on the same soil year after year, particularly the huge monoculture fields of cereals. Repetition of the same crop not only cannot be sustained without lavish applications of petro-chemical based fertilizers, but also allows the pests which live on those crops to flourish in a way which would be impossible with rotation. They have to be killed, as do the weeds which compete for moisture and nutrients. Even with this massive chemical saturation, which grows stronger as the target pests develop resistance, we cannot grow enough food to feed the ever-increasing number of animals and continue to import large amounts of high-protein fodder from the developing world.

The impact of this chemical cocktail is wider than its effect on the fertility of the soil. Some of the nitrogen from fertilizers runs off the land and into rivers, lakes and ponds, where it has precisely the same effect on algae that it has on crops – it fertilizes it. The algae grows rapidly and has the potential to produce toxic 'blooms', just as in the oceans, which can be lethal to all animals, us included. When the plants that overgrow a lake, river or part of the sea die, their remains are broken down by bacteria that take oxygen from the water, suffocating other life. For example in 1981, '83 and '86, numerous flatfish were found dead in the North Sea, where this process had led to an 80 per cent decrease in oxygen in bottom waters.[21] This combination of effects is called 'eutrophication'.

Some nitrogen is washed down into the ground water and eventually into underground reservoirs from which water is extracted for our use. There are now legal limits set – somewhat arbitrarily – for the amount of nitrogen in drinking water because of its association with 'blue baby syndrome', which is a potentially fatal destruction of the red blood cells in newborn children. The nitrogen can also transform into nitrites, which can combine with the proteins in food to form nitrosamines, which are carcinogenic.

Despite this knowledge, there is a tacit admission that the recommended levels of nitrogen in ground water will, at some point, be dramatically exceeded, particularly in the monoculture areas of East Anglia and the Midlands. Quietly and with no publicity, emergency denitrifying water treatment plants have been built for the time when levels rise to alarming proportions. It is entirely consistent with the Government's age-old propensity to treat the symptoms and not the causes.

As it is, drinking water frequently fails to meet the statutory levels and Friends of the Earth estimate that four to five million Britons sometimes drink water containing nitrate pollution higher than the EC safety standards.[22] Even higher levels have been found in mineral waters, even those drawn from the deepest, water-bearing strata. As it can take surface water up to 100 years to percolate down this far, we have obviously not seen the worst of the problem.

The other players in this unsustainable assault on the land are the pesticides – poisons designed to kill weeds, fungi, insects and other life. Many are also directly poisonous to us. They nearly all have alarming aspects, but perhaps the most worrying of all are the organophosphate (OP) pesticides. These are based on the incredibly toxic nerve gases pioneered by Nazi Germany and perfected by the West after the war in combination with the same German scientists who developed them. In their military form, OP pesticides can kill in seconds or lead to permanent disability.

Many of them are currently in use, with sheep dip being one of the most common. This has been used for decades in a totally uncontrolled way against scab and blow fly, despite numerous reports of severe and permanent ill effects on some farmers. The symptoms they experience – dizziness, nausea, double vision, total lethargy – are absolutely consistent with the symptoms of nerve gas poisoning. The compulsory use of sheep dip was dropped in 1995, but it is still in use, with some minor control requirements. Little research has been carried out into its effects on the sheep – who are totally immersed in a tank full of toxic solution.

The Institute of Comparative and Environmental Toxicology, New York, estimates that there are over one million people affected by pesticide poisoning each year, with 20,000 deaths world-wide.[23] In addition, longer term health effects, like cancer and birth abnormalities, are not usually included in these statistics. If they are also taken into account, the situation looks even more grim. Pesticide usage is increasing by 12.5 per cent per year[24] and in 1988 the sales of British Agrochemical Association members totalled just over £1 billion.[25]

It goes without saying that the widespread use of pesticides upsets any concept of natural balance, but perhaps the most concerning aspect is that we simply have no idea what their long-term effects are – and that includes their effect on us, because every single one of us has pesticide residues in our body, even newborn babies. They infiltrate their way into the food chain in a way which concentrates them the higher up the chain they travel. For example, a water bird which lives on fish, which eat small crustaceans, which graze on weeds, which absorb their nutrients from the water which surrounds them, will have concentrations of pesticides in its flesh 80,000 times stronger than the water which started the whole thing off in the first place.[26]

Not quite as dramatic, but based on the same principle, is the example of grazing animals such as cows, which have pesticide concentrations 14 times stronger than the vegetation they eat.[27] The message is clear – the Sunday roast has 14 times more pesticides in it than the potatoes and parsnips which surround it.

The results of pesticide residue tests on meat and dairy

products make frightening reading. In 1988/9, tests of UK-produced beef showed that two in seven samples contained dieldrin.[28] Dieldrin is an insecticide rated 'extremely hazardous' by the World Health Organization at levels above the EC limit. It can cause birth defects and cancer and is very persistent in the environment, being highly poisonous to birds, fish and mammals, including humans.

Dairy products are, however, the main dietary source of the highly toxic organochlorine pesticides – a fact now accepted by the US Government. In 1989, each dairy-eating person in the UK consumed an average of 123 pints of fresh milk and cream and 56 pints of skimmed milk.[29] In 1988, residues of organochlorines were detected in 44 per cent of 120 samples of UK milk.[30] These were below the Government's safety limits. In 22 samples of UK UHT cream, five contained dieldrin.[31]

Another environmental problem which comes from animals, literally, is, to put it bluntly, their propensity to crap a lot. An awful lot, as it happens. The estimate for the US herd alone is 115,420 kilograms a second![32] In Germany, more than three tonnes of liquid manure is produced for every one of its 70 million citizens.[33] In the Netherlands, pork production is a major threat. The 14 million animals in the south excrete so much manure that nitrate and phosphate have saturated surface layers of soil and contaminated water supplies in many areas.[34] And it is the same, to a greater or lesser degree, all over Europe.

The amount of manure now being produced by intensively reared animals is such that the land will simply not absorb it all. So what do we do with it? Rather like nuclear waste, we store much of it and hope it will go away. And some of it does, by leaking into rivers and streams where it can exterminate all life, and by seeping into underground water supplies. We show great concern when similar things happen with human sewage, but this stored animal slurry is 100 times more polluting than our own effluvia.

A process takes place in these slurry storage lagoons which intensifies yet another of the world's great environmental disasters. The large amounts of ammonia in the slurry become a breeding ground for bacteria, which turn it into acid. This then evaporates, combines with nitrous oxide from fertilizers and industrial pollution and forms acid rain.

Across virtually the whole of the northern-most parts of the northern hemisphere, acid rain is souring soil, destroying forests and rendering once prolific waters lifeless. The contribution made by livestock slurry to this intractable destruction is central. In some countries, such as Belgium and Holland, it is the primary cause of the acid rain. In the animal-rearing Pel region of Holland, 97 per cent of the entire forest is dead.[35] In Britain, the highest levels of acid rain are recorded in the intensive dairy-farming counties such as Cheshire, but the effects can be seen all over the north of the country.

In whatever direction you raise your eyes and view the world's horizons, there is environmental collapse. The statistics for the rate of degeneration are shocking, none more so than those which document the spread of deserts. The Sahara, that once fertile region which formed part of the lush granary that supplied the Roman Empire, has extended its sandy fingers southwards into Africa by 320 kilometres in the last 20 years alone.[36] And its progress is accelerating. Like the barren wastes of the Middle East, which were also once lush and verdant, the cause was – and still is – livestock grazing.

As already mentioned, international capital demands the most productive lands for its own interests, so poor people are increasingly pushed onto marginal areas. The grazing of their sheep, goats, cattle and camels there ensures the destruction of the vegetation which could hold the desert at bay. The desert advances and they move on, chopping down more trees to provide more grazing and accentuating the problem.

The climate itself responds as the reduction in water vapour prompts permanent changes in the weather pattern, reducing rainfall levels even further and ensuring there is no quick-fix solution to the problem. The deserts are here to stay. And, according to the United Nations, they're growing at the rate of 207,200 square kilometres annually – an area the size of England and Scotland.[37]

But the problem of desertification is much more widespread and complex than simply the relentless spread of existing deserts. It is increasingly affecting the arid and semi-arid rangelands of the sub-tropics, which girdle one third of the world. The grazing of increasing numbers of cattle is breaking down the soil's structure, reducing its fertility and again making permanent changes to the prevailing weather patterns. The land around established water sources is amongst the most degraded, as cattle are herded here in ever-increasing numbers.

Elsewhere, the swelling human population, continued overstocking and the elimination of grasses which hold the soil together and their replacement by weeds are ensuring that one third of the world's entire surface is rapidly advancing towards becoming desert. As a consequence, the great rivers of Africa – the Senegal, the Chari and the Niger – are beginning to dry out. This has led to the greatest mass migration in world history and by the year 2000, over half of the world's entire population will live in urban areas. The prospect this holds out for the breakdown of social cohesion, for the spread of disease, for the flourishing of abject despair and misery and the blossoming of all the nastier human traits, is really quite dispiriting.

To my mind, one of the most depressing realities of the meat

culture is the refusal of the most addicted country, the
United States, the wealthiest country the world has ever seen,
to respond to the huge problems on its own doorstep. These
rank in importance with many of the developing world's
problems and are, in many instances, responsible for them.

Meat – and by meat I mean beef – is the macho symbol of
American manhood (and womanhood for that matter) and the
eating of it is considered as unassailable a right as the right to
carry arms and kill people with them. The US has exported its
hamburger culture to every corner of the world and, without a
complete revolution in thought and action, stands a very good
chance of destroying it.

Of course, what you see on the surface does not always
reveal the reality beneath. There is an almost awe-inspiring
beauty in the agricultural regions of the Western states of the
Dakotas. The sky seems to extend forever over land on which it
is often impossible to see a human structure, let alone a human.
To stand on elevated ground and see into infinity almost hurts
the imagination. This is the country of Wounded Knee, the
Badlands, the Black Hills, the Sioux nation of Native Americans
– the Ogallala and Rosebud tribes of the Great Plains. It is also a
country of agricultural desolation.

When you fly from Rapid City in South Dakota to Denver,
Colorado, it is in something resembling a cigar tube with two
engines. But the minuscule size of the aircraft means you fly at a
comparatively low height, with the changing landscape clearly
visible below – once you have torn your white knuckles away
from the seat in front.

I was puzzled at first as to why all the cultivated patches
were completely round – as circular as though they had been
drawn with a pair of compasses. Then even I was able to work
out that something was operating from a central pivot – an
automatic weeder, a fertilizing boom, perhaps even a means

of ploughing. What I didn't immediately realize was that every one of the thousands of fields I saw – and there are millions of the same if you include the other states on the same longitude – was a product of automatic irrigation. The circles were created by the booms which dispense water drawn from one huge, natural, underground acquifer. Its name, aptly taken from the Native American, is the Ogallala acquifer.

It was only the presence of this huge source of water which allowed US farmers to turn buffalo pasture into arable land. Now they have drawn so much water from it that the rains cannot replenish it fast enough and much of this artificially fertile land is being lost, returning to its original state as buffalo pasture – but without the buffalo. It took millions of years for Nature to form the Ogallala acquifer and now water tables are dropping and wells going dry. The US Department of Agriculture estimates that at the current rate of water usage, the aquifer may be exhausted in 30 years.[38] If this happens, the High Plains of the US will be uninhabitable to humans. The reason for the decline is the same old story – grazing for cattle, or cereals which are largely to feed to cattle. Every kilogram of beef produced from this grain uses 3,000 litres of disappearing water, many more times the amount needed to produce vegetable foods.[39]

The figures produced by the University of California for that state, where most agricultural land is irrigated, are even more dramatic, placing water use for vegetables such as tomatoes, potatoes and carrots in the 20 to 30 gallon range for an edible pound of food. For beef it is 5,214 gallons.[40] The message is loud and clear: vegetable and fruit production consumes a fraction of the water used for beef cattle, their slaughter and the preparation of the meat they provide. And yet only 2 per cent of the entire US arable land is used for fruit and vegetables. In contrast, 64 per cent is used to produce livestock feed.[41] In the

US, water shortages are already at critical levels with 25 per cent more being taken than replenished.[42]

Fresh water, once a seemingly abundant resource, is now becoming scarce in many regions of the world. Between 1940 and 1980, world-wide usage has doubled and 70 per cent goes to agriculture.[43] In the US, nearly half of all water consumed goes to grow feed for livestock.[44]

But nothing is allowed to threaten the right of the beef producers to carry on producing. When John Robbins wrote his excellent book Diet for a New America (Stillpoint, 1987) and again when Jeremy Rifkin wrote the well-researched Beyond Beef (Dutton, 1992; Thorsons, 1994), both books which catalogued the environmental collapse of the US, they were belittled and attacked by the Cattlemen's Association while the Government simply ignored them.

So the destruction continues. Ten per cent of the publicly owned, arid rangelands of the west have turned to desert[45] while 70 per cent of the remainder were classified by the US Bureau of Land Management in 1990 as in 'an unacceptable condition'.[46]

This love affair with the beef cow is changing and damaging the US beyond recognition. In the twentieth century alone it has lost half its topsoil – the fertile top layer without which almost nothing will grow.[47] And it is continuing to blow and flood from the land at the rate of seven billion tons every year.[48] With luck, through the decay of organic material and the erosion of rock and stones, 2.5 centimetres of topsoil may be produced every 100 years – a losing battle!

Eighty-five per cent of this loss is attributed to livestock rearing[49] and its effect has been to permanently remove from production one third of all arable land.[50] It's probably worth remembering that many previous and great civilizations have tumbled for precisely this reason!

I don't want to bog this book with statistics, but I will

quote just a few more in order to paint clearly the picture of irresponsibility inherent in a meat-based diet. Much is now talked about 'sustainable agriculture' or 'sustainable growth' and the varying amounts of energy expended on producing different types of food show clearly why this talk needs to become a reality.

The total amount of forest cleared in the US for grazing or the production of fodder is 260 million acres.[51] The relationship between meat production and deforestation is so direct that Cornell University economist David Fields and his colleague Robin Hur estimate that for every person who changes to a vegan diet, an acre of trees is spared every year.[52]

Livestock farming also devours fossil fuels. David Pimentel, a specialist in agricultural energy at Cornell, states that 30,000 kilocalories of fossil fuel energy are burned to produce a kilogram of pork in the USA – equivalent to the energy in four litres of petrol. Plant foods are much more efficient. Corn or wheat provide 22 times more protein than feedlot beef. Soya beans are a huge 40 times more efficient.[53]

But before we in Britain show any smug satisfaction at the US picture, it's worth looking at our own country. Five million acres of arable land are threatened with erosion; 80 per cent of our chalk downlands have been destroyed as has 80 per cent of limestone grasslands; half our fens and mires have been drained and 90 per cent of our ponds; nearly half of the tiny amount of remaining ancient woodlands has been cleared since the 1940s and over the same period, enough hedgerow (109,000 miles) has been grubbed out to circle the Earth four times.[54] Along with this has gone a devastation of our flora and fauna. More damage has been done to the British countryside in the last 50 years than in the previous 500, most of it by farmers of meat and dairy products.

Speak to farmers, watch them at work and you will see that most have little interest in the ecology of their land but an awful lot in the money they can make from it – with a few honourable exceptions, of course.

For me, the example which sums up the sad reality of the destruction lies right on my own doorstep. It is a tiny wood no more than 500 metres long and, at its widest, a mere 150 metres, which slopes down a hillside to the River Weaver. To walk through this little patch of shade, to stop and listen, to wait quietly and observe offers endless rewards that enrich me. Rabbits scamper as you approach and on sunlit evenings the red tinge of fox can sometimes be seen trotting between trees. The wood is home to weasels and voles and every kind of mouse and the winter earth reveals the scratchings of badgers looking for cockchafer grubs. Overhead are the huge nest of a heron, the smaller one of a kestrel and hundreds of others. The mocking laughter of a green woodpecker often follows you and the lesser spotted woodpecker is even brave enough to come into the garden. In early summer it is sometimes necessary to cover your mouth with your hand to avoid inhaling insects from the myriad that dart and dash and hover beneath the trees. Bluebells, wood anemones, pink campions, Himalayan balsam, foxgloves and star of Bethlehem take their turn to blossom.

One woodland boundary is the grassy embankment of a canal, beyond which the valley continues but in a very different form. It is a barren wasteland, devoid of every piece of vegetation so that cattle can graze. A few clumps of grass cling to its steep sides, the cattle's hooves having torn most away to expose the sandy soil beneath. At best the field can provide only a few mouthfuls of grazing, but some farmer saw fit to fell everything which once existed here.

The wood that gives me so much pleasure was also once felled, some 30 years ago, but has regenerated itself. I dread

waking to hear once again that most chilling of sounds – the
wavering rasp of a chainsaw as it destroys precious woodland
for a few extra mouthfuls of grazing.

This inexorable destruction both at home and around
the world is encouraged by subsidy, which ensures farmers and
livestock producers make money whatever they do. So they will
go on doing it. In Britain, according to the Ministry of Agriculture, the subsidies for beef, sheep, pig and milk products in
1994 totalled £1.2 billion.[55] In Europe as a whole, they were
more than £100 billion and for fishing, £54 billion.[56] Throughout Central and South America and Africa the story is similar.

Power and control ensure that the wealthy West will be the
last to feel the effects of a dying world. That, unfortunately,
delays the necessary changes in policy required to stem the rot.
But one thing is certain – no one can avoid the eventual
outcome.

The most frightening aspect of this predicted Armageddon
is that the point of no return will be passed long before the final
collapse. When that point will be we can only guess, but you
have the ability to take back control of your life at any time and
make the decisions which are necessary to reverse the decline.
There is one thing within your power which will have a huge
and immediate impact – and that is to change your diet. Stop
eating meat and fish today, give up dairy products, and you
immediately remove yourself from the cycle of exploitation and
destruction. Even better, raise your voice in protest, join with
others such as Viva! and actively fight against the grey men
who will allow greed to destroy the globe.

15 ◆ POLITICAL PERSUASION

Kenya clarified my thinking and in 1993 I decided to leave my job. The next question was whether to continue with the important areas which I felt the Vegetarian Society had abandoned – actively campaigning on farm animal abuse and trying to influence the next generation. I really had no choice and Viva! came into being.

The first, low-key announcement of its existence was made at the World Vegetarian Congress in Holland in August 1994, where I was a speaker. Then, on 26 October 1994, Viva! was launched. All the battles, disappointments, doubts or concerns which had preceded this day evaporated as I looked at the packed room in the Union Club in London's Gerrard Street, in Soho. We had drastically underestimated the numbers who would attend and the anticipated 50 had swelled to nearer 100.

Alongside me as speakers were Michael Mansfield, QC, a Viva! trustee, a friend and a brilliant and principled defence barrister; David Gee, ex-Director of Friends of the Earth; David Ryde, the wonderful vegan GP who served on the medical sub-committee of the British Olympic Association; Jon Wynne-Tyson, the eminent author of works on humane thought and animal rights; *Guardian* writer, author and cookery devotee Colin Spencer; *Darling Buds of May* actress and devoted vegetarian Pam Ferris; and the dreadlocked, kind and gentle poet Benjamin Zephaniah, who read some of his poems to end the launch on exactly the right note of humour and hope.

One person who I would have liked to be there unfortunately couldn't attend. I don't have many heroes or heroines, but one of them is Professor Richard Lacey, the person most responsible for bringing the dangers of bovine spongiform encephalopathy (BSE, commonly known as 'mad cow disease') to the public's attention. He is one of the few academics who does not weigh his career prospects against his beliefs and is brave, fearless and totally principled in an age when all three qualities are in very short supply.

Just for the record, Richard Lacey is a professor of clinical microbiology at a Leeds hospital and also a medical doctor. He has had over 200 papers published and was a Government adviser as a member of MAFF's Veterinary Products Committee until his resignation in 1989. Subsequently, both his professional standing and his sanity have been challenged by Conservative MPs in an obvious attempt to undermine his standing.

Professor Lacey has written that the Government has jeopardized public safety in order to save the livestock industry from ruin and this policy has considerably increased the chances of humans catching the disease. If he is right – and he puts the odds at about 60 per cent – then Britain faces a most frightening epidemic of a fatal and incurable disease – Creutzfeldt Jakob disease (CJD), which is the human version of BSE. CJD has been known about for some years but hit the news in 1986 when cattle were diagnosed with a similar disease which attacks the nervous system and turns the brain into a sponge-like substance, honeycombed with holes. By 1995 it had spread to at least 150,000 cows.[1]

The most baffling aspect of the story is the agent which causes BSE and possibly also the CJD infection – it has never been identified. It is neither a virus nor a bacterium and has broken all the most basic rules of biology. It appears to be able to alter its form, one minute being inanimate and capable of withstanding enormously high temperatures, while another minute being active and highly infectious. It is so infectious that some doctors have refused to perform autopsies on those who have died from CJD and some hospitals have declined to admit people believed to be infected with it. Any prospective cure lies at the very limits of current science.

With extraordinary short-sightedness, in August 1988 the Government offered farmers only half the market value for cows diagnosed with BSE. Not surprisingly, the number of reported cases remained comparatively low, but when the compensation was increased to the full value of the animal in February 1990, the number shot up. You don't have to be Einstein to work out the reason why.

The youngest cow so far to develop BSE was 18 months old and the oldest 18 years.[2] The incubation period in humans can be as long as 30 years, so any apparent failings in Government policy are unlikely to show up for an election or two. The link between cows and humans has yet to be proved but the Communicable Disease Surveillance Centre reported that people who regularly eat veal or beef products are 13 times more likely to die of CJD than those who don't.[3] Professor Lacey is convinced that CJD and BSE are one and the same disease.

In May 1988, the Government set up the Southwood committee, charged with the task of investigating BSE. The committee contained no experts on the subject and didn't consult any. Despite this, it eventually instructed that all infected cattle should be slaughtered. But the action came too late – meat from over 600 obviously diseased cows had already found its way into the shops.[4]

This figure was eventually made to look like chicken

feed by a Granada TV's *World in Action* documentary programme, 'The Hidden Epidemic', transmitted in October 1995.
It revealed that secret Government papers admitted that for
every cow diagnosed with BSE at least another two infected
cattle were entering the food chain.[5] Microbiologist Dr Stephen
Dealler estimates that by the year 2001, 1.8 million infected
cattle will have been eaten, ensuring that the majority of the
British population will have eaten beef or beef products from
BSE infected cattle.[6]

Despite their apparent lack of expertise, the Southwood
committee produced other recommendations and reassurances.
They said that the risk of humans catching the disease through
what they ate was remote, seemingly ignoring the fact that it
was from feed that cows themselves had first caught it. They
thought that the sheep encephalopathy called scrapie had
passed to cattle in their feed when sheep offal, including brains,
had been rendered down and turned into a high-protein supplement. Professor Lacey, however, is not convinced by this
scenario and believes that a similar process of turning cow
body parts into feed may have triggered the infection, which
he thinks may have always been present in cattle. Certainly it
was this which caused the disease to spread so rapidly.

However, the Southwood committee also concluded that
there was no risk of mother cows passing the disease on to their
calves. Just as important, they were convinced that cows would
prove to be 'dead end hosts' and would not pass BSE on to other
species. Had they been sufficiently inquisitive they would have
known that even as they were writing their report, animals
other than cows had already been infected with BSE. Their
reassurance that cows would not infect their calves was also
later to be proved conclusively wrong.

The report concluded: '...if our assessment of these likeli-
hoods is incorrect, the implications would be extremely serious.'[7]

The Southwood committee's final recommendation advocated the formation of another committee to carry out more research. This second committee, the Tyrrell, published its report in early 1990[8] and recommended that brains of *all* slaughtered cattle, whether they were showing symptoms or not, should be checked for BSE. It also proposed that all cases of CJD should be monitored for 20 years.

Both these recommendations would seem to be both logical and necessary. Monitoring of all slaughtered cattle would obviously show if the disease were widespread amongst animals not showing symptoms and monitoring human cases would show if there were any increase in CJD. But the Government has failed to act on either recommendation.

As already mentioned, the cause of BSE in cattle was initially thought to be the practice of rendering meat and carcasses to produce high-protein animal feeds. In 1988 this was banned, but there was little effect on the ballooning statistics. The number of new cases rose from 500 in January 1989 to 900 in December 1989. Exactly one year later the figure rose to 1,500 *a month*.[9] Another of the predictions in the Southwood report had been that the disease would peak at 400 cases a month...

In May 1990, a domestic cat died from BSE but the Government refused to acknowledge the fact. By July, however, 52 cats had been infected[10] and the Government had to admit that pet food containing beef was probably the cause. The question now was how many other species were at risk and whether humans were one of them.

In the following year, 1991, we started to find out. Numerous tests and studies on other animals had been conducted and seven out of eight species of mammals which were fed infected meat developed the disease.[11] This was later to increase to 18 species. They included pigs and monkeys. Reports also came in of a puma and a cheetah dying of BSE. In a pronouncement of sublime complacency, MAFF then announced that the disease would peak that year and would disappear altogether by 1994.

By the end of 1992, the number of reported cases had risen to 25,025[12] and the disease showed no signs of abating. It was obvious that as the apparent source – infected animal feed – had been banned, some other transmission route was at work. The evidence pointed to vertical transmission – mother cows passing it on to their calves. The Government still refused to admit this until in 1994 the number of cases rose to 137,000, six times greater than Southwood's worst case scenario.

However, the admission was retracted a year later and MAFF maintained that the reason for the continuing outbreaks of BSE was the illegal use of banned slaughterhouse products – 'specified offal' – in vitamin and feed supplements which found their way into fish and other meals. If you were a cynic, you might believe this about-face has something to do with protecting the export of veal calves to Europe. Who would buy and eat veal believed to be infected with BSE? If humans can catch CJD from cattle, Britain has ensured that Europe shares this frightening prospect with us.

Despite having been consistently wrong on almost everything else, the Government continues to insist that the infection is restricted to the nervous system and is not present in the flesh of animals. Removing the brains, spinal column, spleen, thymus gland and tonsils makes beef safe to eat. But cells from all these organs enter the blood and find their way to other organs, including the liver and bones – and bones are the principal source of gelatine, made through a process of concentration. Knowing that the agent can withstand incredibly high temperatures, Professor Lacey's fear is that gelatine may turn out to be a particularly potent source of infection. Its widespread use in dozens of prepared foods, from confectionery to aspic, jellies to pork pies, makes that possibility extremely disturbing.

These fears were given a chilling boost by an extraordinarily detailed and technical seven-page article in the *Mail on Sunday Review* of 17 December 1995. Entitled 'Mad Cow Disease and Human Deaths – A New Link' and written by Peter Martin, it traced a path of Governmental complacency and apparent deception surrounding the two diseases. The first clue that CJD and BSE might be linked, it seemed, was established by neuro-pathologist Dr Robert Perry and clinical virologist Dr Harash Narang in 1989 after examining two CJD cases. Narang, then a Government scientist with the Public Health Service Laboratory (PHSL), went on to develop a comparatively simple test for diagnosing sub-clinical BSE in cattle which hadn't yet shown symptoms of the disease but which would end up in the food chain.[13] We now know from the large number of cases which fall into this category, estimated by Dr Stephen Dealler to be 1.5 million by 2001,[14] that the cost of full compensation would be enormous – in the region of £1.4 billion. The Government chose not to use the test.

Dr Narang tried to get funding for his test and in 1990 received a rejection from MAFF, despite having proved the test successful at the Central Veterinary Laboratory at Weybridge at the end of 1989. Also in 1990, the House of Commons Agriculture Committee asked for submissions from scientists on the dangers of BSE, including two written requests to Narang. According to the *Mail on Sunday*, these requests were never passed to Narang by his superiors. Eventually he was contacted by phone. What he told the committee was disturbing.

He stressed the need for urgency and explained that his test would cut the time necessary for the results of infectivity studies from between one and three years to just 20 days. On the question of BSE posing only a remote risk to humans, as claimed by the Government, Narang is reported to have said that, compared to other encephalopathies, BSE was a unique superstrain with an unusually short incubation time – half that of sheep scrapie. He maintained that because 23 different species of animal had died from BSE, this indicated that humans were not totally resistant to it. Again MAFF turned down his test, as did the Ministry of Health.

With the onset of the BSE epidemic, the nature of CJD appeared to change. Before 1985, CJD tended principally to attack the cerebral cortex and sometimes the cerebellum. In 1995, the *Mail on Sunday* claimed to have discovered six recent cases of CJD, chosen randomly, in which the infection had taken a different course. It had principally attacked the central grey matter of the brain and the cerebellum. This is exactly what happens in the brains of cattle infected by BSE!

Another change in CJD appears to be the young age at which some victims were being diagnosed – three teenagers in Britain and four others world-wide. Again, Dr Narang believes this could be as a result of intravenous infection in children through the sockets of lost milk teeth.

Dr Narang's trail of discovery became somewhat disrupted in 1991 when the PHSL accused him of failing to register his work under new health and safety regulations. His work obviously fell outside the scope of the new Health and Safety Executive (HSE) regulations which were to safeguard against genetic manipulation which was dangerous to humans. However, in 1992, he was suspended by the PHSL following complaints of alleged professional misconduct in obtaining patients' notes improperly.

The complaint was still hanging over Dr Narang in 1993 when the PHSL instructed him to leave his specially equipped laboratory in Newcastle and go to work in London. An ex-MAFF employee was put in as his assistant and in his absence, the PHSL destroyed a number of his valuable spongiform samples. The end came in 1994 when Dr Narang was made redundant.

This abridged newspaper report is a remarkable
document, not least in its detail. It reveals that possibly the
most knowledgeable man in Britain on the subject of BSE, the
one person who holds the key to its understanding, its diagnosis
and its possible future course is – 'redundant'. Dr Narang was
also, of course, one of the few scientists able to challenge the
Government's oft repeated challenge that beef is safe to eat.

At the time of writing, in 1996, the furore surrounding BSE
has died down, but there is a sense of waiting to see what will
happen next. Four dairy farmers who had infected cattle in their
herds are known to have died from CJD. Also, in May 1994,
Vicky Rimmer, a 15-year-old girl, was diagnosed as having CJD
and diet was thought to have been the cause. Proper tests will
not be possible until after her death. One of the most disturbing
aspects of this sad case was reported in the *Daily Mirror* on 25
January, 1994. It claimed that Vicky's mother maintains that a
doctor from the CJD surveillance unit examined her daughter
and asked Mrs Rimmer not to make the case public. 'Think of
the economy and the Common Market,' he is reported to have
said. If this report is true, then of all the rallying cries with
which people have faced death, this probably ranks as one
of the most banal and insulting.

We still know almost nothing about BSE and the Government's handling of the outbreak indicates that its primary
concern throughout has been to protect the beef and dairy
industries. To that end it has gambled with human safety.

Don't dismiss this as an isolated incident. In 1990, the US
administration admitted that a new virus had become widespread in the country's cattle herd. This bovine immunodeficiency-like virus (BIV) is the cattle equivalent of AIDS and a
member of the same family of lentiviruses.

It was only a question of time before the infection arrived

in Britain and it happened in 1993. The first outbreak was in a herd of Holstein dairy cows just 10 miles from my home. MAFF's attitude to it was predictable. BIV was, they said, a mild infection which, like all lentiviruses, was extremely slow in producing symptoms. It posed no threat to cattle and there was no need to make it a notifiable disease. Above all, it was species specific and could not infect humans. In other words, business as usual.

Unfortunately, the facts didn't fit the theory. The farmers who had the outbreak, Tim and Linda Blything, had bought some new cows from Holland and within days of arriving on the farm they had all gone down with a whole range of diseases. Days later the rest of their herd followed. By pure luck, their local vet had just returned from the US and suspected BIV. He informed MAFF.

Suddenly confusion and contradiction engulfed the Blythings. Samples were taken, visitors arrived and departed, tests were done and undone. There was a whole series of admissions and denials, followed by counter denials and counter admissions, but no diagnosis.

Meanwhile, almost every pregnant heifer aborted as she approached full term and most calves which were born lasted only a day or two. One minute they were suckling, the next they looked ill and by the following day they were dead. Within a few months, over half the herd had either died or had been destroyed to save suffering. Still MAFF refused to diagnose BIV and continued to insist that BIV was, in any case, a benign infection.

The moment the words 'cow AIDS' started to be attached to the Blythings' herd, they were virtually finished in the locality. Deliverers didn't want to deliver, neighbours didn't want to be neighbourly and no one wanted to touch their cattle. Although they could have officially sold their stock, no one locally would buy them and the Blythings felt it would be irresponsible to take them elsewhere and sell them secretly.

After a few months the symptoms largely subsided in the remaining herd, but when the cows approached full-term pregnancy again, the same distressing deaths started to happen once more.

When I visited the farm towards the end of 1994, some cattle lay almost motionless, exhibiting almost total lethargy. Calves were equally depressed, with discharges from the eyes. Most of the cattle had lost huge amounts of body tissue and looked like skeletons, particularly around the hind quarters. And as one cow was herded into the milking parlour she showed similar symptoms to those associated with BSE – she was extremely nervous and jumpy and on the point of panic. As MAFF still refused to accept that BIV was the cause, I decided to carry out my own research.

The virus was first discovered in a cow in Louisiana in 1969 when it was looked at with only mild interest, frozen and forgotten. It was labelled R29, the number of the cow from which it was taken. With the outbreak of human HIV and AIDS, suddenly interest perked up and the virus was defrosted and cloned hundreds of times over in the belief that it might provide an understanding of the human disease.

Few scientific papers had been published on BIV, but two early ones showed success in infecting human cells.[15] Early work also indicated that the effect on cattle was not quite so benign as MAFF has maintained. All subsequent laboratory experiments, however, showed it wasn't virulent and wouldn't infect human cells. Something didn't add up!

All experimental work, I discovered, had been carried out on the one and only R29 sample which had been cloned so many times that it had become extremely weak, indicating that the later tests were probably valueless. What was disturbing was a discovery which showed that BIV, too, could jump species – to rabbits, sheep and goats – both *in vivo* and *in vitro*.[16]

The man who had originally identified BIV in the US was Professor Gene Luther of the University of Louisiana. He flew to Britain in July 1994 to inspect the Blythings' herd and study the post-mortems on the dead cattle. He disagreed with much that he read and was in no doubt as to what afflicted the cattle – BIV. He also disagreed with MAFF's insistence that BIV was a benign infection, citing the US experience.

In the private report he prepared for the Blythings, he set out his own experiences. He wrote that herds in Oklahoma and Texas had accidentally been infected with BIV in 1991 by a contaminated commercial vaccine. It resulted in abortions, infertility in both heifers and bulls, chronic wasting, diarrhoea, pneumonia, lameness, mastitis and unexplained deaths – an almost exact catalogue of the Blythings' problems. Professor Luther had kept track of one of these herds and by 1994 it had been reduced to two animals, the remainder having died or been destroyed – an outcome which was far from benign.

At his own university in Louisiana, the 139-strong herd were all descendants of the original poor old R29 and in 1989 80 per cent were BIV positive. Three years later only 12 of them were still alive. Death of the calves born to this herd was almost total.

The professor also followed a US beef herd for three years when it was kept on open pastures with little or no stress. All the cattle appeared to prosper and flourish, apart from occasional bouts of depression and nervousness. But after they had been slaughtered he discovered that every single animal had brain lesions, swelling of the brain, meningitis and enlarged lymph nodes. They were very sickly cattle.

A copy of Professor Luther's report was presented to MAFF towards the end of 1994. As a consequence MAFF sent a delegation out to Louisiana to interview him. During

this visit, Professor Luther stressed to the delegation that
the outbreak of BIV at the Blythings' farm presented a unique
opportunity. He advised that the farm should be turned into
one enormous laboratory in which it would be possible to study
BIV, in particular this newly mutated and seemingly virulent
version of the virus. He was left with the impression that this
was what would happen. It didn't!

Professor Luther is convinced that BIV acts in a similar
way to HIV. By depressing the cow's immune system, a whole
range of unrelated diseases is allowed to flourish. One of the
key factors which leads to the cow showing symptoms appears
to be stress – milking, pregnancies, crowded living conditions,
calving and transportation. When the cows are left to their own
devices, grazing on open pasture, the symptoms subside but
the disease remains.

The main difference between the US and British
experience was the speed with which the disease had developed
in Cheshire. It was no longer a lenti (slow) virus but an amazingly quick one. What had happened to the infection in its
passage across the Atlantic? It seemed that a new, more
virulent form of the virus was at work.

I unearthed some recent US research which did, in fact,
show that the BIV virus has developed substantial genetic vari-
ation, that is to say, it has changed its form dramatically.[17] But
even more worrying was an indication that it is considerably
more complex than other lentiviruses, providing it with an
almost endless ability to mutate. There was also the suggestion
that different diseases are combining together, enabling each
to prosper. One of these is the cow leukaemia virus – BLV.

Following this path, I went to Belgium in August 1994
to see Professor Arsen Burney at Jambloux, an agricultural
university. He is a specialist in BLV. He was forthright in his
opinions and spoke openly to me:

Governments are against research into animal diseases. They don't want to pay compensation and so they ignore them until it's impossible not to. There is a general attitude surrounding BIV and that is that it's better not to ask questions. The truth is that we can't ignore it any longer.

There is a great danger that nature is beginning to strike back. Cramming millions of birds into one shed, imprisoning 3,000 pigs in one building, pushing cattle to the brink of their ability to cope is simply not sustainable. We are creating huge problems which are likely to be insoluble. We are creating perfect breeding grounds, we are abusing antibiotics and the result is already a disaster for the animals and it is likely to be a disaster for humans also.

In this instance, if BIV does result in a weakened immune system, and the evidence points to the fact that it does, then we can never say that it cannot pass from cows to humans. I am not convinced that BIV will not infect humans. It is possible for any virus to jump to humans, it just depends upon the circumstances.

Professor Burney's expression 'we are abusing antibiotics' started me down another path. The Blythings believe the cattle they bought from Holland were, in fact, falsely ear tagged and originated from Eastern Europe. It is coming to light that the conditions in which animals are kept there are much worse even than in Britain and very high stocking densities lead to an even greater use of antibiotics. It is known with human HIV that a history of antibiotic use increases the risk of infection and makes the disease progress faster. A similar effect could be happening in cattle.

It is impossible to tell yet whether BIV is a direct threat to humans or not. Most of those working in the field think not – but with such a rapidly mutating virus, however, all future bets must be off.

But there is another, real and immediate threat which Professor Arsen Burney can see quite clearly:

Because of the weakened immune system in cattle with BIV, the other diseases they suffer from will prosper and many of these will pass to humans.

Professor Richard Lacey was in total agreement when I asked him to comment on this:

About half the infections which affect cattle also affect humans. If a cow's immune system is weakened, and that's precisely what appears to be happening, then it is inevitable that it will produce something harmful to us. People don't die of AIDS, they die of a whole range of illnesses and infections brought on by the reduced immune system. And that is what will happen with BIV. What we are particularly at risk from are salmonella 0517, tuberculosis, listeria, staphylococcus, cryptosporidium and numerous viral complaints and abscesses.

Perhaps it's no accident that the diseases which look like prospering are the very infections which are increasingly failing to respond to antibiotics.

One thing is certain – if BIV does pose a threat, either directly or indirectly, MAFF has guaranteed that it is now endemic in the UK herd.

When the story first broke, Tim Blything received several

phone calls from farmers who believed their stock had also contracted BIV. None of them cared to leave a telephone number. I managed to track down two of them.

The cattle of both farmers had symptoms identical to the Cheshire herd, but because of MAFF's refusal to regard the disease as anything out of the normal, to make it notifiable and pay compensation, both sold their stock on the open market and they are now distributed amongst other herds.

MAFF has stuck to its position throughout, but not so Milk Marque, the privatized version of the Milk Marketing Board, which refused to accept milk from the Cheshire herd because they were not satisfied that BIV is destroyed by pasteurization.

The main point is that another potentially devastating disease has appeared in cattle and again our leaders have placed commercial concerns above those of either human or animal health.

On March 20, 1996, the day this chapter was to go to press, the British Government was forced into a humiliating U-turn. It confirmed that there is a new form of CJD which is caught from eating beef. The public sense of betrayal was huge.

So, Narash Narang was right all along. Prof. Richard Lacey was also vindicated when a government expert, Prof. John Pattison, confirmed that his prediction of a possible 500,000 human deaths each year may be correct. It is a grim commentary on modern society and a frightening validation of this book.

16 ◆ THE END IS NIGH...

There is a sense of society having reached a watershed. Disenchantment with politicians is almost absolute and few people have any belief in their ability to be truthful or to solve the overwhelming problems which confront us, some of which I have written about in this book.

We in the West have had two centuries or more of raping the rest of the world in order to bolster our way of life. We are surrounded by the legacy of that conduct. The centres of our large cities are places where brutality is squeezing out hope and where aspirations are being smothered at birth. Sub-cultures of disinterest and despair blossom where hope has been extinguished. The quest for knowledge and understanding has been subverted into a production line of industrial and commercial fodder.

With the exception of a privileged minority, which has a vested interest in wealth and power, it is almost impossible to find anyone who believes that we have discovered any answers to the questions of survival. Our continuance on this globe is in doubt because of greed, but still the only philosophy on offer is one of selfishness and individuality.

As a consequence, an armoury of laws and military tactics has been prepared for use against those who will never be amongst the favoured; to control those who express their frustrations in anger on the streets.

This is why the protesters against live exports offer encouragement to all of us. There is not one shred of self-interest in their actions, simply a heart-felt cry to place concern and care above the right to make profits. It is an eddy of hope in the middle of a powerful tide bearing us all towards an increasingly unsustainable future.

Part of this future is the new 'salvation' of genetic engineering. It is the latest in a long line of 'miracles' – nuclear energy, antibiotics, the green revolution – and just as all these had a dramatic downside, so will engineering experimentation. It's just that no one is prepared to admit it.

The first acknowledgement of genetic 'success' was the granting of the very first patent for a life form at Harvard University in 1992.[1] It was the oncomouse. This little creature was bred to develop cancer after only six weeks of life and immediately became a commodity for sale to vivisection laboratories, saving them the task of having to induce cancer in their own mice.

A whole string of similar experiments is taking place across the world. I've already mentioned the Belgian Blue cow *(see page 84)*. Meanwhile, in the Swiss Brown cow, a gene has been deliberately activated to trigger a brain disease to which they're susceptible. The reason is that cows which suffer from the disease naturally tend to have an increased milk yield. The US Department of Agriculture produced transgenic lambs with added growth hormone. Their fate was to develop degeneration of the liver and kidneys which was believed to have been caused by a form of diabetes. Other experimenters repeated the process with almost the same results. All the lambs involved in the experiment died of their diseases before they were 12 months old.[2]

Experiments are also taking place to introduce a tobacco gene into sheep to act as an insect repellent and ward off blow-fly strike.[3]

Perhaps the most repellent experiment which has so far come to light took place in 1985 in the US when human growth hormones were introduced into a pig – the Beltsville pig.[4] This poor creature was stricken with arthritis and when it tried to walk it could only crawl around on its knees. Most of the time it simply lay still, obviously stressed and in pain, incapable of fighting off a whole range of diseases which afflicted it. Despite this travesty, the Beltsville pig was capable of reproduction – but so far we have not been told what happened to its offspring.

The same National Cancer Institute, producer of the Beltsville pig, is still at it, playing creator with a range of animals, the latest of which is the supermouse. Cancer manifests itself by the uncontrolled growth of cells and they have used this fatal tendency to try and produce faster-growing food animals. Using a human gene which is linked to the growth of cancerous cells, they have, they claim, produced a mouse which grows to twice the normal size.[5] They have not revealed their failures.

This gene is now being tried in pigs and although the results are secret, the BBC2 documentary Meat, transmitted in May 1995, indicated that the creatures suffer severe muscle wasting.[6] In order to forestall public concern about the use of a cancer gene in human food, it has been renamed a 'growth' gene.

The same TV documentary revealed that in Israel, they have identified the gene which causes chickens' necks to be scraggy and featherless and the one responsible for causing feathers to curl. By combining the two in experimental chickens they have produced a near-bald bird, its bare flesh exposed by the remaining curly feathers. And all so they can build broiler sheds in the inhospitable heat of the Negev desert.[7]

All across the world, multinational agribusinesses have spent billions on developing animal and vegetable products and thousands of patents are pending. We know nothing of these corporations' work, its failures and implications, but the products are on the way. They will come onto the market and be bought by an unsuspecting public, for the British Government, for one, has no intention of requiring labelling. So far in the UK only the Co-op has broken ranks and intends to label the food it sells as having been 'genetically modified'.

Experimenters are playing with the 100 or so genes they have managed to map in complex animals which contain millions of genes, most of which are a total mystery to them. They have no idea what will be the result of mixing, matching and introducing entirely foreign genes.

So we can look forward to a future in which animals, including humans, will be the players in a huge improvised drama with no script and no known ending. The cast could include hairless pigs, sheep with even hairier coats, hibernating sheep, asexual cattle, pigs with cat leukaemia genes and vegetables with fish genes. The encore might well be vegetables that produce meat-like substances from animal genes – at least that is the intention.

The West's stranglehold on the developing world will strengthen with the production of seeds that can only be grown with specific pesticides, ensuring even greater control over others' agriculture and economies.

None of this, of course, has anything to do with feeding the starving of the world. Companies cloak their experiments with expressions of hope for the developing world, but these are the same people who could end world famine today if they so wished. Instead, the huge development expenditure will be recouped through high prices, ensuring that the products are placed out of reach of those who need feeding the most.

Anyway, who needs a six-legged chicken which tastes of asparagus or an 80kg cauliflower that can whistle?

Around the globe, the conditions for warfare have been created as land, water and food, the basic requirements of life, start to diminish. And the only solution on offer is the policy which created these conditions. A restrospective view of the last few decades should send a chill running through us all because our path into the future will be charted from the same stars, the twinklings of an imploding society. The people who have made such a mess claim the right, the perception and the ability to solve the world's problems. It's like giving the National Front responsibility for race relations.

Perhaps the simplest and most easily understood indicator that our current leaders have got it wrong is their insistence that we are all motivated by our wallets. There are hundreds of millions of vegetarians in the world and not one is motivated by money. Some are concerned about health, others are appalled by the squalid exploitation and slaughter of animals, for some it is the environment which is the main issue and for the others the exploitation of developing countries. For most, it is a mixture of all these reasons.

Certainly the protesters who blockaded the ports of Brightlingsea, Dover and Shoreham and Coventry airport in all weathers did not first feel for their wallets; neither do the Viva! supporters who stand handing out leaflets and rattling tins for hours on end in high streets across the country; neither do the children who have flocked to our nationwide marches and spoken words to fill our eyes with tears and our hearts with hope.

This might be the start of a great movement for change. Certainly, such a simple and effective choice has rarely confronted people. By changing your diet you can take the first step in allowing the planet to breathe again, allowing the healing process to start. There is nothing else under your control that can immediately ease the destruction of the environment and begin to correct the impoverishment of the world's poor. There is nothing else that can so effectively improve your own health and there is certainly nothing else that will have such an influence on ending the barbarous existence to which so many animals are subjected.

Compassion is one of the greatest human traits and it has been diminished to the point of frailty. If our children are to grow and prosper then we must reassert it and we must be aware that it is incompatible with our present society. Changing the world has to start with first changing ourselves and then the system under which we live.

Contact Viva! at
PO Box 212
Crewe
CW1 4SD
UK

◆ REFERENCES

INTRODUCTION

1　D. Pimentel, *Food, Energy and the Future of Society*, Wiley, 1979, p.26

2　L. R. Brown, ed., *State of the World 1990*, Worldwatch Institute, 1990, p.4
F. Moore Lappe, *Diet for a Small Planet*, Ballantine Books, 1982, p.69

3　C. R. W. Spedding, *Food for the 90's: The impact of organic foods and vegetarianism*, 1990, pp.231–41

4　M. L. Burr and P. M. Sweetnam, 'Vegetarianism, dietary fibre and mortality', *The American Journal of Clinical Nutrition*, 36, 1982, pp.873–7
M. L. Burr and B. K. Butland, 'Heart disease in British vegetarians', *The American Journal of Clinical Nutrition*, 48, 1988, pp.830–2
J. Chang-Claude *et al.*, 'Mortality pattern of German vegetarians after 11 years of follow-up', *Epidemiology*, 3, 1992, pp.395–401
D. A. Snowdon, R. L. Philips and G. E. Fraser, 'Meat consumption and fatal ischaemic heart disease', *Preventative Medicine*, 13, 1984, pp.490–500

5　Chang-Claude, op. cit.

M. Thorogood *et al.*, 'Risk of death from cancer and ischaemic heart disease in meat and non-meat eaters', *British Medical Journal*, 308, 1994, pp.1667–70

6   P. Cox, *Peter Cox's Guide to Vegetarian Living*, Bloomsbury, 1995

7   J. Potter, 'How vegetables fight cancer', *Living Earth and Food Magazine*, January–March 1995, pp.8–9

8   The Ministry of Agriculture, Fisheries and Food, United Kingdom, *Slaughter Statistics*, London, 1994

CHAPTER 1: THROUGH THE EYES OF A PIG

1   CRB Research (formerly The Scottish Farm Buildings Investigation Unit), *Does Close Confinement Cause Distress in Sows?*, A review of the scientific evidence commissioned by the Athene Trust, July 1986, p.6

2   A. B. Durning and H. B. Brough, *Taking Stock: Animal farming and the environment*, Worldwatch paper 103, Worldwatch Institute, Washington, DC, July 1991, p.11

3   'How to make $12,000 sitting down', *Farm Journal*, August 1966 J. Robbins, *Diet for a New America*, Stillpoint, New Hampshire, 1987, pp.82–3

CHAPTER 2: THE CHICKEN AND THE EGG

1   M. J. Gentle *et al.*, *Applied Animal Behaviour Science*, 27, 1990, pp.149–57
M. J. Gentle, 'Beak trimming in poultry', *World's Poultry Science Journal*, 42, 1986, pp.268–75
M. J. Gentle, 'Pain in birds', *Animal Welfare*, 1, 1987, 4
P. Grigor *et al.*, 'Effect of beak trimming on the growth and behaviour of turkeys', *Veterinary Record*, 18 March 1995

2   N. G. Gregory and L. J. Wilkins, 'Broken bones in domestic fowl: handling and processing damage in end-of-lay battery hens', *British Poultry Science*, 30, 1989, pp.555–62

3   M. C. Appleby, *Do Hens Suffer in Battery Cages?*,
    A review of the scientific evidence commissioned by
    the Athene Trust, Institute of Ecology and Resource
    Management, University of Edinburgh, October 1991, p.2
    Figures for the UK also taken from a poultry industry
    show on 'The Structure of the Industry' table; Royal Show
    at Stoneleigh, 1992
    The Farm Animal Welfare Network, *Hidden Suffering*,
    1993, p.4

4   Appleby, op. cit.
    M. R. Baxter, 'The welfare problems of laying hens in
    battery cages', *The Veterinary Record*, 11 June 1994

5   The Ministry of Agriculture, Fisheries and Food, United
    Kingdom, *Slaughter Statistics*, London, 1994

6   The Ministry of Agriculture, Fisheries and Food, United
    Kingdom, *Codes of Recommendation for the Welfare of
    Livestock: Domestic fowls*, MAFF Publications, 1992, p.11

7   C. Whitehead, of the Agricultural and Food Research
    Council and of the Institute of Animal Physiology and
    Genetic Research at Roslin, Lothian, on *Horizon*, BBC2 TV,
    'Fast Life in the Food Chain', 18 May 1992

CHAPTER 3: THE SIX-WEEK LIFECYCLE

1   'Broiler losses reach high levels in winter months', *Poultry
    World*, May 1994, p.13. These figures are from an estimate
    by John Parsons, the National Farmers' Union poultry
    specialist and editor of *The Broiler's Bulletin*.

2   '£10m study into battery chicken deformities',
    The Independent, 13 March 1992
    'Bone defects found in most fast-growth oven chickens',
    The Guardian, 13 March 1992

3   J. Webster, Head of the Department of Animal Husbandry, Bristol University, on *Horizon*, BBC2 TV, 'Fast Life in the Food Chain', 18 May 1992

4   The Farm Animal Welfare Council, *Report on the Welfare of Broiler Chickens*, The Ministry of Agriculture, Fisheries and Food Publications, April 1992, p.3

5   The Ministry of Agriculture, Fisheries and Food, United Kingdom, *Slaughter Statistics*, London, 1990–4

6   T. W. Lippman, *The Washington Post*, 26 November 1982

7   J. Robbins, *Diet for a New America*, Stillpoint, New Hampshire, 1987, p.53

8   *Poultry World*, p.28, November 1985

9   *Horizon*, op. cit.
     'The price of meat', *The Sunday Times Magazine*, 12 November 1989
     Communication with the British Poultry Meat Federation, July 1992
     C. Druce, *Chicken and Egg: Who pays the price?*, Green Print, 1989

10   *Horizon*, op. cit.

11   Channel 4 TV, *Undercover Britain*, 'This Turkey Business', 19 December 1995

12   Ibid.
     The Ministry of Agriculture, Fisheries and Food, *Slaughter Statistics*, op. cit.

13   I. Duncan *et al.*, 'Assessment of pain associated with degenerative hip disorders in adult male turkeys', *Research in Veterinary Science*, 30, 1991, pp.200–3
     H. Pearce, 'The farm fresh turkey scandal', *Environment Now*, December 1989, pp.10–11
     Undercover Britain, op. cit.

14   *Horizon*, op. cit.

15   *Undercover Britain*, op. cit.

16 Ibid.
17 J. Webster, *Animal Welfare: A cool eye towards Eden*, Blackwell Science, 1995

CHAPTER 4: THE END OF THE LINE

1 P. Stevenson, *The Welfare at Slaughter of Broiler Chickens*, Compassion in World Farming Trust, 1993, p.6
2 Ibid., p.3

CHAPTER 5: SCIENCE, SADISM AND SALVATION

1 PETA, *Unnecessary Fuss* video, 1984
2 PETA, *Britches* video, 1986

CHAPTER 6: MILKY BAR KIDOLOGY

1 E. Brunner, *Bovine Somatotropin: A product in search of a market, details on BST*, The Food Commission, 1988, p.21
   M. Hornsby, 'A British side of beef', *The Times Saturday Review*, 3 October 1992
2 P. Jackson, Head of Farm Animals Division, Cambridge Veterinary School, on 'Fast Life in the Food Chain', *Horizon*, BBC2 TV, 18 May 1992
3 Ibid.
4 Ibid.
5 Ibid.
6 United States Department of Agriculture, *People on the Farm: Dairying*, 1981
7 W. B. Faull and R. Murray, R., *Farmer's Weekly*, 17 September 1993
8 J. Webster, *Animal Welfare: A cool eye towards Eden*, Blackwell Science, 1995

9   The Ministry of Agriculture, Fisheries and Food, United
    Kingdom, *Lameness in Dairy Cattle*, MAFF Publications,
    1992, p.5
10 Webster, op. cit.
11 'Fast Life in the Food Chain', *Horizon*, BBC2 TV,
    18 May 1992
    The Ministry of Agriculture, Fisheries and Food, United
    Kingdom, personal communication, June 1992
12 F. W. Abbey, *Feeding and Breeding of Dairy Cows in the USA*,
    Nuffield Farming Scholarships Trust, 1990, p.3
13 *Horizon*, op. cit.
14 Ibid.
15 Brunner, op. cit., p.11
16 P. Willeberg, 'Bovine Somatotropin and clinical mastitis:
    Epidemiological assessment of the welfare risk', *Livestock
    Production Science*, 36, 1993, pp.55–66
17 Brunner, op. cit.
18 The Ministry of Agriculture, Fisheries and Food, Veterinary
    Medicines Directorate, *Bovine Somatotropin Update*,
    January 1995
19 'Business Bulletin', *The Wall Street Journal*, 16 March 1995
20 *Milk: Not a natural*, PETA, Washington, DC, 1995
21 'Imports contain banned BST, claims producer', *Farming
    News*, 2 June 1995

CHAPTER 7: A TALE OF THE SEA

1   United Nations Food and Agriculture Organization, *State
    of the World: Fisheries and Aquaculture*, Rome, March 1994
2   Ibid.
    'Catastrophe threatens world's fisheries as stocks fall',
    The Guardian, 12 March 1994
    'Fish Wars', *Panorama*, BBC1 TV, 5 February 1996

3   Greenpeace, *Net Losses, Gross Destruction, European Fisheries in Crisis*, June 1992
    International Council for the Exploration of the Seas, *Report of Industrial Fisheries Working Group*, March 1992
4   *The Guardian*, op. cit.
5   EU, *Quality Status Report on the North Sea*, December 1993
6   *The Guardian*, op. cit.
7   Ibid.
8   J. Ashworth, *Fishing News*, 17 February 1989
9   *The Guardian*, op. cit.
10 Greenpeace, *North Sea: Invisible decline*, April 1994
    United Nations Food and Agriculture Organization, op. cit.
11 F. J. Verheijen and R. J. A. Buwalda, *Pain and Fear of Hooked Carp in Play*, State University of Utrecht, May 1988
12 R. Aronson, 'Rise and fall of life at sea', *New Scientist*, 29 September 1990
13 '30,000 sea birds starved to death', *The Guardian*, 16 February 1994
    M. Avery and M. Robins, 'Seabirds for fish: A deadly trade-off', *New Scientist*, 16 March 1991
14 Greenpeace, op. cit.
15 'Crisis for cod and haddock threatens fish and chips', *The Guardian*, 3 June 1995
    'Lack of action on overfishing threatens North Sea cod stocks with oblivion', *The Guardian*, 8 June 1995
16 United Nations Food and Agriculture Organization, op. cit.
17 'Saving the sea', *The New Internationalist*, August 1992
18 Greenpeace, op. cit.
19 'Lousy fishing blamed on salmon farmers', *The Financial Times*, 6 August 1992
20 The Ministry of Agriculture, Fisheries and Food Consumer Panel, *Chemicals Used in Fish Farming and their Control*, July 1995

21 'Salmon in shops to be tested for pesticides',
    The Daily Telegraph, 8 July 1992
22 H. Kane, 'Growing fish in fields', *World Watch*,
    September/October 1993, pp.20–7
23 Ibid.
24 D. Brown, 'Salmon suffer painful deaths on fish farms',
    The Daily Telegraph, 13 May 1991
25 *The New Internationalist*, op. cit.
26 Ibid.
    N. Lenssen, *Worldwatch Reader*, ed. L. Brown, W. W.
    Norton & Co., 1991
27 The Environmental Investigation Agency, *The Potential
    Impact of Ultraviolet-B Radiation on the Antarctic Marine
    Ecosystem*, June 1992
28 *The New Internationalist*, op. cit.

CHAPTER 8: NOT SO FREE RANGE

1   The Ministry of Agriculture, Fisheries and Food,
    Agriculture in the United Kingdom 1993, HMSO, 1994
2   Ibid.
3   A. Tyler, *Silence of the Lambs*, Animal Aid, 1995
4   D. Henderson, of the Animal Research Diseases Research
    Association, Edinburgh, and past President of the Sheep
    Veterinary Society, on his video, *Lamb Survival*, Farming
    Press
5   *Wool Manufacturing: Shear pain*, PETA, Washington, DC,
    1995
6   The Ministry of Agriculture, Fisheries and Food, 'Fox
    predation on lambs', statement to League Against Cruel
    Sports, 17 February 1994
7   'Survey of predation on lambs by foxes', *The Field*,
    April 1993, p.56
8   G. Coles, *The Sheep Farmer*, March 1995, p.1

9   The Farm Animal Welfare Council, *Report on the Welfare of Sheep*, MAFF Publications, April 1994, p.22

10 Animal Liberation Australia, *This Bloody Disgrace is Called Mulesing*, New South Wales, 1992

11 The Ministry of Agriculture, Fisheries and Food, *Agriculture in the United Kingdom 1994*, HMSO, 1995

12 The Farm Animal Welfare Council, op. cit., p.5

13 Farmline, *Cattle Feeding Concentrates in Fewer, Larger Lots*, US, June 1990

14 S. Hughes, 'Planning row for first UK feedlot', *Big Farm Weekly*, 2 November 1989

15 J. D'Silva, 'Of cows, calves and culls', *The Vegan*, Autumn 1991, pp.6–7

16 J. Webster, Head of Animal Husbandry at Bristol University, on 'Fast Life in the Food Chain', *Horizon*, BBC 2 TV, 18 May 1992

17 P. Street, Head of the Department of Agriculture at Reading University, ibid.

18 Ibid.
    R. McNally and P. Wheale, *Animal Genetic Engineering*, Pluto Press, London, 1995

19 Street, op. cit.

CHAPTER 9: TRANSPORTS OF DESPAIR

1   Compassion in World Farming, *For a Few Pennies More* video, 1994

2   P. Stevenson, *A Far Cry from Noah*, Green Print, 1994, p.102

3   Ibid., p.73

4   *Eurogroup Report, 1992, Dossier to the UK Presidency of the EC: Farm animals sent for slaughter across Europe*, 9 July, 1992

5   Ibid.

6   Compassion in World Farming, 'The Long Distance
    Transport of Animals', 1995
7   Stevenson, op. cit.
8   Directive 91/628/EEC paragraph 1, chapter 1, of the
    Directive's Annex
9   Stevenson, op. cit.
10 Compassion in World Farming, *The Road to Misery* video, 1992
11 The Ministry of Agriculture, Fisheries and Food, personal
    communication to J. Gellatley, 8 February 1996
12 Stevenson, op. cit.
13 'Ministers shoot down Europe's game bird ruling',
    The Times, 13 January 1996
14 T. G. Knowles *et al.*, 'Long distance transport of lambs
    and the time needed for subsequent recovery',
    Veterinary Record, 133, 1993, 286–93
15 The Ministry of Agriculture, Fisheries and Food news release,
    22 June 1995
16 R. Ewbank, *Welfare problems in calf transportation*,
    Universities Federation for Animal Welfare, 1986
17 Scientific Veterinary Committee, *Report of the Working
    Group 'Transport of farm animals and pets' of the Scientific
    Veterinary Committee, Section: Animal Welfare*, Brussels,
    30 April 1992
18 Commission's Report attached to a Proposal for a
    Council Directive amending Directive 91/628/EEC on the
    protection of animals during transport, July 1993
19 The Ministry of Agriculture, Fisheries and Food,
    *Report of the working party evaluation of 'Export health
    certification procedures'*, March 1994
20 Ibid.
21 Ibid.
22 Ibid.
23 'The Veal Trail', *Dispatches*, Channel 4 TV, 17 January 1996

CHAPTER 10: MEAT TO DIE

1   N. G. Gregory et al., 'Effects of CO_2 on man', Fleischwirt, 70, 1990, pp.1173–4

2   N. G. Gregory, 'Preslaughter handling, stunning and slaughter', Proceedings of the 38th international congress of meat science and technology, 1, 1992, pp.27–34
    R. Hoenderken, Proceedings of the CEC seminar on stunning of animals for slaughter, Martinus Nijhoff, Boston, 1983

3   The Royal Society for the Prevention of Cruelty to Animals, The Slaughter of Food Animals, 1985

4   M. H. Anil, 'Studies on the return of physical reflexes in pigs following electrical stunning', Meat Science, 30, 1991, pp.13–21

5   The Ministry of Agriculture, Fisheries and Food, Code of Practice on the Welfare of Red Meat Animals at Slaughter, MAFF Publications, 1992

6   Anil, op. cit.

7   The Farm Animal Welfare Council, Report on the Welfare of Livestock (Red Meat Animals) at the Time of Slaughter, MAFF Publications, 1984

8   M. H. Anil, 'Current developments in the stunning and slaughter of pigs', Pig Veterinary Journal, 26, 1991, pp.85–93

9   N. G. Gregory and S. B. Wotton, 'Sheep slaughtering procedures – I: Survey of abattoir practice', British Veterinary Journal, 140, 1984, pp.281–6

10 N. G. Gregory and S. B. Wotton, 'Sheep slaughtering procedures – II: Time to loss of brain responsiveness after exsanguination or cardiac arrest', British Veterinary Journal, 140, 1984, pp.354–60

11 M. H. Anil et al., 'Increased vertebral artery blood flow following neck sticking in slaughter calves', Paper at conference of the Association of Veterinary Teachers and Research Workers, Scarborough, 1992

12 P. Stevenson, *The Welfare of Pigs, Cattle and Sheep at Slaughter*, Compassion in World Farming Trust, 1993, p.9

13 The Farm Animal Welfare Council, op. cit.

14 C. C. Daly and P. E. Whittington, 'A survey of commercial practices used in the stunning of cattle', *The Times*, 23 February 1990

15 *File on Four*, BBC Radio 4, February 1995, quoted Department of Health statistics
J. Erlichman, 'Most British chickens are "poison risk"', *The Guardian*, 6 October 1994
A Consumers Association survey also states that one third of chickens are infected with salmonella, 5 October 1994

16 *Meat*, BBC2 TV, 9 May 1995

17 Communicable Disease Reports, Communicable Disease Surveillance Centre, reports for 1995

18 K. Jones and D. Telford, 'On the trail of a seasonal microbe', *New Scientist*, 6 April 1991, p.36
R. Lacey, *Hard to Swallow*, Cambridge University Press, 1994, p.169

19 *Meat*, op. cit.

20 Jones and Telford, op. cit., campylobacter underreported by 10 to 100 times
Lacey, op. cit., reporting figures from the Communicable Disease Reports for 1991, Communicable Disease Surveillance

21 *Meat*, op. cit., MAFF's Veterinary Products Committee conducted the tests

22 Ibid.

23 *File on Four*, op. cit.

24 G. Cannon, *Superbugs: Nature's revenge*, Virgin Publications, 1996

25 Ibid.

26 R. Lacey, *Stop Bugging Me*, Viva!, 1995, p.6

CHAPTER 11: AN APPLE A DAY

1   M. Hornsby, 'Gummer goes tooth and claw for vegetarians', *The Times*, 2 May 1990

2   M. Thorogood *et al*, 'Risk of death from cancer and ischaemic heart disease in meat and non-meat eaters', *British Medical Journal*, 1994, 308, pp.1667–70

3   Ibid.

4   Ibid.

5   Ibid.

6   Ibid.

7   British Nutrition Foundation annual report and accounts, 1993–4, p.7

8   British Medical Association, *Diet, Nutrition and Health*, BMA Report, 1986, p.49

9   P. Cox, *Peter Cox's Guide to Vegetarian Living*, Bloomsbury, 1995, quoting *The Independent*, 23 October 1990, p.155

10 R. B. Mazess, 'Bone mineral content of North Alaskan Eskimos' *The American Journal of Clinical Nutrition*, 27, (9), 1974, pp.916–25

11 'Challenge to US habits – major Chinese study backs plant based diet', *Herald Tribune*, 10 May 1990

12 C. D. Nielsen *et al.*, 'Effect of dietary boron on mineral, estrogen and testosterone metabolism in post-menopausal women', *FASEB J*, 1, (5), 1987, pp.394–7

13 British Medical Association, op. cit.

14 T. Sanders *et al.*, 'Haematological studies on vegans', *The British Journal of Nutrition*, 40, (9), 1978, pp.9–14

15 S. Moncada *et al.*, 'Symposium on regression of atherosclerosis', *European Journal of Clinical Investigation*, 23, 1993, pp.385–98
    W. Willett and F. M. Sacks, 'Chewing the fat – how much and what kind', *The New England Journal of Medicine*, 324, 1991, pp.121–3

16 J. Burslem *et al.*, 'Plasma apoprotein and lipoprotein lipid
    levels in vegetarians', *Metabolism*, 27, 1978, pp.711–19
    M. Fisher *et al.*, 'The effect of vegetarian diets on plasma
    lipid and platelet levels', *International Medicine* 146, 1986,
    pp.1193–7
    D. B. Hunninghake *et al.*, 'The efficacy of intensive dietary
    therapy alone or combined with lovostatin in out patients
    with hypercholesterolemia, *The New England Journal of
    Medicine*, 328, 1993, pp.1213–9
    F. M. Sacks. *et al.*, 'Plasma lipoprotein levels in vegetarians:
    the effect of ingestion of fats from dairy products', *JAMA*,
    254, 1985, pp.1337–41
    R. O. West and O. B. Hayes, 'Diet and serum cholesterol
    levels: a comparison between vegetarians and non-
    vegetarians in a Seventh-Day Adventist group', *The American
    Journal of Clinical Nutrition*, 21, 1968, pp.853–62
17 F. Pixley *et al.*, 'Effect of vegetarianism on development of
    gallstones in women', *British Medical Journal*, 291, 6 July
    1985, pp.11–12
18 Cox, op. cit., quoting *The Lancet*, 24 August 1990
19 B. Spock, D. Ornish, W. C. Roberts *et al.*, 'Recommended
    revisions for dietary guidelines for Americans', submitted
    to the Dietary Guidelines Advisory Committee, Department
    of Agriculture and Department of Health & Human Services,
    31 January 1995
20 J. Chang-Claude *et al.*, 'Mortality pattern of German
    vegetarians after 11 years of follow-up', *Epidemiology*, 3,
    1992, pp.395–401
21 American Cancer Society, *Cancer Facts and Figures, 1993*,
    American Cancer Society, 1993
22 G. Block, 'Epidemiologic evidence regarding vitamin C
    and cancer', *American Journal of Clinical Nutrition*, 54,
    1991, pp.1310S–14S

E. Negri *et al.*, 'Vegetable and fruit consumption and cancer risk', *International Journal of Cancer*, 48, 1991, pp.350–4

23 British Heart Foundation, *UK Heart Statistics*, 1994

24 M. L. Burr and B. K. Butland, 'Heart disease in British vegetarians', *The American Journal of Clinical Nutrition*, 48, 1988, pp.830–2

25 M. Thorogood *et al.*, 'Plasma lipids and lipoprotein cholesterol concentrations in people with different diets in Britain', *British Medical Journal, Clinical Research Edition*, 295 (6594), 8 August 1987, pp.351–3

26 American Heart Association, *1992 Heart and Stroke Facts*, Dallas

27 M. L. Burr and P. M. Sweetnam, 'Vegetarianism, dietary fibre and mortality', *The American Journal of Clinical Nutrition*, 36, 1982, pp.873–7
    M. L. Burr and B. K. Butland, 'Heart disease in British vegetarians', *The American Journal of Clinical Nutrition*, 48, 1988, pp.830–2
    J. Chang-Claude *et al.*, 'Mortality pattern of German vegetarians after 11 years of follow-up', *Epidemiology*, 3, 1992, pp.395–401
    D. A. Snowdon, R. L. Phillips and G. E. Fraser, 'Meat consumption and fatal ischaemic heart disease', *Preventative Medicine*, 13, 1984, pp.490–500

28 O. Lindahl *et al.*, 'A vegan regime with reduced medication in the treatment of hypertension', *British Journal of Nutrition*, 52, 1984, pp.11–20

29 D. Ornish *et al.*, 'Can lifestyle changes reverse coronary heart disease?', *The Lancet*, 336 (8708), 21 July 1990, pp.129–33

30 T. C. Campbell *et al.*, *Study on Diet, Nutrition and Disease in the People's Republic of China*, Cornell University, 1989

31 *US Dietary Guidelines*, USDA, federal advisory committees nutritional recommendations to Secretaries of Agriculture, Health and Human Services, 1995, p.21
32 *The Facts about Antioxidants: How they impact health and disease*, Solgar Nutritional Research Centre, 1996, p.3

CHAPTER 13: DEVELOPED TO DEATH

1   Third World Guide, Instituto del tercer mundo, Uruguay, 1991/2
2   Ibid.
3   World Health Organization, *Bridging the Gaps*, 1995
4   G. Lean *et al.*, *Atlas of the Environment*, Arrow Books, 1990
    E. F. Trainer, *Abandon Affluence*, Green Print, 1985
5   Lean, op. cit.
6   P. A. Yotopoulos, *The 'New' Food-Feed Competition*, FAO Animal Production and Health paper 63, FAO, Rome, 1987, p.24
7   A. B. Durning and H. B. Brough, 'Reforming the livestock economy', *State of the World 1992*, Worldwatch Institute, 1992, p.69
8   L. Brown *et al.*, *State of the World 1990*, Worldwatch Institute, 1990
9   The Ministry of Agriculture, Fisheries and Food, United Kingdom, *Slaughter Statistics*, London, 1994
10 A. Moyes, *Common Ground*, Oxfam, 1985
11 G. Yates, *Food: Need, greed and myopia*, Earthright Publications, 1986, p.16
12 Yotopoulos, op. cit.
13 Ibid.
14 Yates, op. cit.
15 D. and M. Pimentel, *Food, Energy and Society*, Edward Arnold, 1982
16 Ibid.

17 C. R. W. Spedding, Food for the 90's: The impact of organic foods and vegetarianism, 1990, pp.231–41

18 C. Tickell, speaking at the British Association for the Advancement of Science, 26 August 1991, reported in *The Independent*, 27 August 1991

19 Moyes, op. cit.

20 L. R. Brown, *The Changing World Food Prospect: The nineties and beyond*, Worldwatch paper 85, Worldwatch Institute, October 1988, p.5

21 Tickell, op. cit.

22 Worldwatch Institute, *State of the World 1994*, quoted in 'Overcrowding points to global famine', *The Guardian*, 15 August 1994

23 Office of Technology Assessment, *Technologies to Sustain Tropical Rainforest Resources*, US Congress, OTA-F–214, Forest resources, March 1984, pp.96–7

24 J. Rifkin, *Beyond Beef*, Thorsons, 1994, p.148

25 FAO of the UN, *Trade and Commerce 1989 Yearbook*, FAO, Rome, 43, p.29

26 Rifkin, op. cit., pp.148–9
Associacao Promotora de Estudas da Economica, A Economica Brasil-eira e suas Perpectives, Apecao XXIX, 1990 (Rio de Janeiro: APEC 1990), p.5

27 World Health Organization, *Bridging the Gaps*, 1995

28 Ibid.

29 Ibid.

30 Brandt, W. *North South*, Pan (London), 1980

CHAPTER 14: A MATTER OF ENVIRONMENT

1 G. Lean et al., 'Britain's vanishing forests', The Observer/World Wide Fund for Nature Special Report, 1992

2 E. Goldsmith *et al.*, *The Earth Report 3*, Mitchell Beazley, 1990, pp.70–1

3 Friends of the Earth, *Tropical Rainforests*, FOE, July 1990
4 Ibid.
5 C. Bird, 'Medicines from the rainforest', *New Scientist*, 17 August 1991, pp.34–9
6 Caufield, C., *In the Rainforest*, Picador (London), 1985
7 World Rainforest Movement, Rainforest Destruction: Causes, effects and false solutions, WRF, Malaysia, 1990, p.45
8 Ibid.
9 Ibid.
10 A. B. Durning, 'Fat of the land: Animals' agenda', October 1991, pp.16–20, reprinted from *The Worldwatch Magazine*, Worldwatch Institute, 1991
11 Ibid.
12 S. Boyle and J. Ardill, *The Greenhouse Effect*, New English Library, 1989, p.29
13 J. Gribbin *et al.*, 'The methane mill', *BBC Wildlife*, 7 (6), 1989, p.387
14 Boyle, op. cit.
15 F. Pearce, *Turning Up the Heat*, Paladin, 1989, p.169
16 Quoted in ibid, p.168
17 Boyle, op. cit.
   Gribbin, op. cit.
   Intergovernmental Panel on Climactic Change (IPCC), *Supplement*, February 1992
   Pearce, op. cit.
18 The Soil Association, *Soil Erosion in Britain*, 1986
19 The Ministry of Agriculture, Fisheries and Food, *Agriculture in the United Kingdom 1994*, HMSO, 1995
20 The Soil Association, *Pesticides under our Skin*, 1990
21 The Marine Conservation Society, *Nutrients, Algal Blooms and Plankton*, 1994
22 F. and P. Craig, *Britain's Poisoned Water*, Penguin Books, 1989, p. 24

A. Lees and K. McVeigh, *Pesticides in Drinking Water*, Friends of the Earth, 1990

23 N. Dudley, *This Poisoned Earth*, Piatkus, 1987, p.1

24 Ibid.

25 A. Watterson, *Pesticides and your Food*, Green Print, 1991, p.3

26 The British Medical Association, *Pesticides, Chemicals and Health*, 1991

27 R. Elliot, *The Green Age Diet*, Fontana, 1990

28 Craig, op. cit.

29 Watterson, op. cit.

30 Ibid.

31 Ibid.

32 D. Pimentel, 'Energy and land constraints in food protein production', *Science*, 21 November 1975; states that the livestock of the USA produces 20 times as much excrement as the human population of the USA

33 *Meat Devours Man*, ARD TV, Germany, 1978

34 A. B. Durning and H. B. Brough, 'Reforming the livestock economy', *State of the World 1992*, Worldwatch Institute, 1992, pp.66–82

35 J. G. M. Roelofs, of the Agricultural University Wageningen, on *Meat Devours Man*, ARD TV, Germany, 1978

36 UN Environment Programme, *Sands of Change*, Environment Brief No.2

37 Ibid.

38 W. Lagrone, 'The Great Plains' in Schertz *et al.*, *Another Revolution in US Farming?*, USDA, ESCS, Agricultural Economic Report 441, December 1979

39 A.B. Durning and H.B. Brough, *'Taking Stock; Animal Farming and the Environment'*, Worldwatch Paper 103, Worldwatch Institute, July 1991, p.18

40 'Water requirements for Food Production', University of California Cooperative Extension, 1991, pp.13–17

T. Aldridge *et al.* 'Soil and Water', Fall 1978, p.38

P. and A. Erlich, *Population, Resources, Environment*, WH Freeman, 1972, pp.75–6

41 USDA, 'Agricultural Statistics', 1989

J. Robbins, *Diet for a New America*, Stillpoint, New Hampshire, 1987

42 J. Rifkin, *Beyond Beef*, Thorsons, 1994

43 W. H. Corson, ed., *Global Ecology Handbook*, Beacon Press, Boston, 1990

44 Rifkin, op. cit., p.219

45 Harold Dregne, Professor of Soil Science, University of Texas, quoted in A. B. Durning, 'Fat of the land', Animals' Agenda, October 1991, reprinted from *The Worldwatch Magazine*, Worldwatch Institute, Washington, DC, 1991

46 US Department of the Interior, Bureau of Land Management, 1990, quoted ibid.

47 US Department of the Interior, Bureau of Land Management, *State of the Public Rangelands*, 1990

48 Robbins, op. cit.

49 Robin Hur, quoted in F. Moore Lappe, *Diet for a Small Planet*, Ballantine Books, 1982

50 D. Pimentel *et al.*, 'Land degradation: Effects on food and energy resources', *Science*, October 1986

51 R. Hur, 'Are high-fat diets killing our forests?', *Vegetarian Times*, February 1994

52 Ibid.

53 A. B. Durning and H. B. Brough, 'Reforming the livestock economy', *State of the World 1992*, Worldwatch Institute, 1992, pp.66–82

D. Pimentel, 'Energy and land constraints in food protein production', *Science*, 21 November 1975

54 G. Lean, 'Green and ruined land, vandal farmers' *The Observer* special report, September 1991

55 The Ministry of Agriculture, Fisheries and Food, United Kingdom, *Agriculture in the UK 1994*, HMSO, 1995

56 'Crisis for cod and haddock threatens fish and chips', *The Guardian*, 3 June 1995

CHAPTER 15: POLITICAL PERSUASION

1 S. F. Dealler and J. T. Kent, 'BSE: An update on the statistical evidence', *British Food Journal*, 97, 8, 1995, 3–18

2 R. W. Lacey, *Mad Cow Disease: The history of BSE in Britain*, Cypsela Publications Ltd, 1994

3 R. W. Lacey, *How Now, Mad Cow*, Viva! guide no. 3, 1995, p.5

4 Ibid.

5 'The Hidden Epidemic', *World in Action*, Granada TV, 13 October 1995

6 Dealler, op. cit.

7 R. Southwood, Report of the working party on bovine spongiform encephalopathy, MAFF Publications, 1989

8 D. A. J. Tyrrell, Consultative committee on research into spongiform encephalopathies: Interim report, MAFF and the Department of Health, 1989

9 Dealler, op. cit.

10 R. W. Lacey, *Mad Cow Disease*, op. cit.

11 Dealler, op. cit.

12 Ibid.

13 P. Martin, 'Mad cow disease and human deaths – a new link (mad cow deceit)', *Mail on Sunday Review*, 17 December 1995, pp.20–26

14 Dealler, op. cit.

15 J. A. Georgiades, *Journal of General Virology*, 38, 1978, p.375
J. Grote, Journal of the Royal Society of Medicine, 81, 1988 p.620,

16 J. Brownlie *et al.*, 'Bovine immunodeficiency-like virus – a potential cause of disease in cattle?', *The Veterinary Record*, 19 March 1994, pp.289–91

17 M. A. Gonda, *The Lentiviruses of Cattle*, '*The Retroviridae*', vol. 3, Plenum Press, 1994

CHAPTER 16: THE END IS NIGH

1 R. McNally and P. Wheale, eds., *Animal Genetic Engineering: Of Pigs, Oncomice and Men*, Pluto Press, 1995, pp.151–3

2 Ibid.

3 Ibid.

4 D. Bolt *et al.*, 'Improved animal production through genetic engineering: Transgenic animals', *Proceedings of forum Veterinary Perspectives on Genetically Engineered Animals*, AVMA, 1988, pp.58–61

5 *Meat*, BBC2 TV, 16 May 1995

6 Ibid.

7 Ibid.

◆ BIBLIOGRAPHY

SELECTED READING LIST

Adams, C. J., *The Sexual Politics of Meat*, Polity Press, Cambridge, 1990

Appleby, M. C., *Do Hens Suffer in Battery Cages?*, A review of the scientific evidence commissioned by the Athene Trust, Institute of Ecology and Resource Management, University of Edinburgh, October 1991

Boyle, S. and Ardill, J., *The Greenhouse Effect*, New English Library, London, 1989

Brien, T., *Gene Transfer and the Welfare of Farm Animals*, Compassion in World Farming Trust, August 1995

The British Medical Association, *Pesticides, Chemicals and Health*, London, 1991

Brown, L. R., ed., *State of the World 1990* to *1995* annually, Worldwatch Institute, Washington, DC

Brown, L. R., *The Changing World Food Prospect: The nineties and beyond*, Worldwatch paper 85, Worldwatch Institute, Washington, DC, October 1988

Brunner, E., *Bovine Somatotropin: A product in search of a market, details on BST*, The Food Commission, 1988

Bull, D., *A Growing Problem: Pesticides and the Third World poor*, Oxfam, Oxford, 1982

Cannon, G., *Superbugs: Nature's revenge*, Virgin Publications, London, 1996

—, *The Politics of Food*, Century, London, 1988

Carson, R., *Silent Spring*, Penguin Books, London, 1988

Caufield, C., *In the Rainforest*, Picador, London, 1984

Clements, K., *Why Vegan*, Heretic Books, London, 1995

Clough, C. and Kew, B., *Animal Welfare Handbook*, Fourth Estate, London, 1993

Coleman, V., 'Betrayal of trust', *European Medical Journal*, Devon, 1994

—, 'Food for thought', *European Medical Journal*, Devon, 1994

—, 'Power over cancer', *European Medical Journal*, Devon, 1996

Cox, P., *Why You Don't Need Meat*, Thorsons, Wellingborough, 1986

—, *The New Why You Don't Need Meat*, Bloomsbury, London, 1994

—, *Peter Cox's Guide to Vegetarian Living*, Bloomsbury, London, 1995

Craig, F. and P., *Britain's Poisoned Water*, Penguin Books, London, 1989

Crawford, M. and Marsh, D., *The Driving Force: Food in evolution and the future*, Mandarin, London, 1991

CRB Research (formerly The Scottish Farm Buildings Investigation Unit), *Does Close Confinement Cause Distress in Sows?*, A review of the scientific evidence commissioned by the Athene Trust, July 1986

Davidson, J. and Myers, D., *No Time to Waste: Poverty and the global environment*, Oxfam, Oxford, 1992

Diamond, J., *The Rise and Fall of the Third Chimpanzee*, Vintage, London, 1992

Dobson, A., *The Green Reader*, Andre Deutsch, London, 1991

Druce, C., *Chicken and Egg: Who pays the price?*, Green Print, London, 1989

D'Silva, J. and Stevenson, P., *Modern Breeding Technologies and the Welfare of Farm Animals*, Compassion in World Farming Trust, July 1995

Dudley, N., *This Poisoned Earth*, Piatkus, London, 1987

Duffy, M., *Men and Beasts: An animal rights handbook*, Paladin, London, 1984

Durning, A. B. and Brough, H. B., *Taking Stock: Animal farming and the environment*, Worldwatch paper 103, Worldwatch Institute, Washington, DC, July 1991

—, 'Reforming the livestock economy', *State of the World 1992*, Worldwatch Institute, Washington, DC, 1992

Eckholm, E., *Losing Ground: Environmental stress and world food prospects*, W. W. Norton & Co., New York, 1986

Ehrlich, P. and A., *The Population Explosion*, Arrow Books, London, 1991

Elliot, R., *The Green Age Diet*, Fontana, London, 1990

Elton, B., *Stark*, Sphere, London, 1990

—, *This Other Eden*, Pocket Books, London, 1993

The Farm Animal Welfare Network, *Hidden Suffering*, Huddersfield, 1993

—, *Today's Poultry Industry*, Huddersfield, 1995

Fiddes, N., *Meat: A natural symbol*, Routledge, London, 1992

Gellatley, J., *The Livewire Guide to Going, Being and Staying Veggie*, The Women's Press, London, 1996

Gold, M., *Living without Cruelty*, Green Print, London, 1988

—, *Animal Rights*, Jon Carpenter Publishing, Oxford, 1995

Goldsmith, E. *et al.*, *The Earth Report 2*, Mitchell Beazley, 1990

Goldsmith E., *The Way: An ecological world view*, Rider, London, 1992

Greenpeace, *North Sea: Invisible decline*, April 1994

Gruen, L. *et al.*, *Animal Liberation: A graphic guide*, Camden Press, London, 1987

Harrison, P., *The Third Revolution: Environment, population and a sustainable world*, I. B. Tauris & Co. Ltd, London, 1992

Instituto del tercer mundo, *Third World Guide*, Uruguay, *1991/1992* and *1993/1994*

Lacey, R., *Unfit for Human Consumption*, Souvenir Press, London, 1991

—, *Hard to Swallow*, Cambridge University Press, Cambridge, 1994

—, *Mad Cow Disease: A history of BSE in Britain*, Cypsela Publications Ltd, Jersey, 1994

Lean, G. *et al.*, *Atlas of the Environment*, Arrow Books, 1990

—, 'Britain's Vanishing Forests', *The Observer/World Wide Fund for Nature Special Report*, 1992

Lees, A. and McVeigh, K., *Pesticides in Drinking Water*, Friends of the Earth, London, 1990

McNally, R. and Wheale, P., *Genetic Engineering: Catastrophe or utopia?*, Harvest Wheatsheaf, Hemel Hempstead, 1988

—, *Animal Genetic Engineering*, Pluto Press, London, 1995

Masson, J. and McCarthy, S., *When Elephants Weep: The emotional lives of animals*, Vintage, London, 1996

Meadows, D. *et al.*, *Beyond the Limits*, Earthscan Publications, London, 1992

Mellanby, K., *Can Britain Feed Itself?*, Merlin Press, London, 1975

Melville, A. and Johnson, C., *Cured to Death*, New English Library, London, 1982

The Ministry of Agriculture, Fisheries and Food, *Agriculture in the UK 1994*, annually published, HMSO, London, 1995

Moore Lappe, F., *Diet for a Small Planet*, Ballantine Books, New York, 1982

Moran, V., *Compassion, the Ultimate Ethic: An exploration of veganism*, Thorsons, Wellingborough, 1985

Moyes, A., *Common Ground*, Oxfam, 1985

Newkirk, I., *Save the Animals: 101 easy things you can do*, Angus and Robertson, London, 1991

Pearce, F., *Acid Rain*, London, 1987

—, *Turning Up the Heat*, Paladin, London, 1989

Physicians Committee for Responsible Medicine, *Recommended Revisions for Dietary Guidelines for Americans*, PCRM, 31 January 1995

Pimentel, D., *Food, Energy and the Future of Society*, Wiley, New York, 1979

Pimentel, D. and M., *Food, Energy and Society*, Edward Arnold, 1982

Rifkin, J., *Beyond Beef*, Penguin, New York, 1992; revised edition Thorsons, 1994

Robbins, J., *Diet for a New America*, Stillpoint, New Hampshire, 1987

The Royal Society for the Protection of Animals, *The Slaughter of Food Animals*, 1985

Sharpe, R., *The Cruel Deception: The use of animals in medical research*, Thorsons, Wellingborough, 1988

—, *Science on Trial: The human cost of animal experiments*, Awareness Books, Sheffield, 1994

Spedding, C. R. W., *Food for the 90's: The impact of organic foods and vegetarianism*, 1990

Spencer, C., *The Heretic's Feast: A history of vegetarianism*, Fourth Estate, London, 1994

Singer, P., *Animal Liberation*, Thorsons, London, 1991

Spiegel, M., *The Dreaded Comparison*, Heretic Books, London, 1988

Stephens, F. and Shehata, S., eds, *The Siege of Shoreham: Reflections from the frontline*, Hatagra Ltd, Brighton, 1995

Stevenson, P., *The Welfare at Slaughter of Broiler Chickens*, Compassion in World Farming Trust, January 1993

—, *The Welfare of Pigs, Cattle and Sheep at Slaughter*, Compassion in World Farming Trust, August 1993

—, *For Their Own Good*, Compassion in World Farming Trust, October 1994

—, *The Welfare of Turkeys at Slaughter*, Compassion in World Farming Trust, December 1995

Trainer, F. E., *Abandon Affluence*, Green Print, London, 1985

Trainer, T., *Developed to Death: Rethinking Third World development*, Green Print, London, 1989

Tyler, A., *Silence of the Lambs*, Animal Aid, Tonbridge, 1995

Viva! (Vegetarians International Voice for Animals), *Viva! Guides on 12 Vegan/Vegetarian Issues*, Crewe, 1994

Watterson, A., *Pesticides and your Food*, Green Print, London, 1991

Webster, J., *Animal Welfare: A cool eye towards Eden*, Blackwell Science, 1995

World Health Organization, *Bridging the Gaps*, 1995

World Rainforest Movement, *Rainforest Destruction: Causes, effects and false solutions*, WRF, Malaysia, 1990

Worldwatch Institute, *Worldwatch Magazines*, Washington, DC

Wynne-Tyson, J., *Food for a Future*, Centaur Press, Arundel, 1985

—, *Extended Circle*, Centaur Press, Arundel, 1990

—, *Anything within Reason*, Oakroyd Press, Potters Bar, 1994

—, *Sealskin Trousers and Other Stories*, Oakroyd Press, 1994

Yates, G., *Food: Need, greed and myopia*, Earthright Publications, 1986

SELECTED TV DOCUMENTARIES

ARD TV, *Meat Devours Man*, Germany, 1978

BBC1 TV, 'One Man's Meat', *Heart of the Matter*, 17 November 1991

—, 'Cow AIDS', *Close Up North*, 19 May 1994

—, 'Fish Wars', *Panorama*, 5 February 1996

BBC2 TV, 'Patenting Animals', *Antenna*, 13 December 1989

—, *A Fate Worse than Debt*, 28 December 1989

—, 'Factory Farming and Food Poisoning', *This Week*, 12 July 1990

—, 'Fast Life in the Food Chain', *Horizon*, 18 May 1992

—, *Meat*, over four weeks starting 9 May 1995

Channel 4 TV, *The Animal's Film*, 1982

—, *This Food Business*, 8 August 1989

—, 'Pandora's Lunch Box', *Critical Eye*, 11 September 1990

—, 'Bad Meat Trail', *Dispatches*, 17 October 1990

—, *Patenting Life*, 15 January 1991

—, *The Price of Salmon*, 21 July 1991

—, 'This Turkey Business', *Undercover Britain*, 18 December 1995

—, 'The Veal Trail', *Dispatches*, 17 January 1996

Granada TV, 'Beef Baron', *World in Action*, 13 May 1991

—, 'What Killed Stephen?', *World in Action*, 14 August 1995

—, 'The Hidden Epidemic', *World in Action*, 13 October 1995

SELECTED VIDEOS

Animal Aid, *Their Future in your Hands*, Tonbridge, 1991

—, *Here's the Catch: Poultry catching*, Tonbridge, 1993

—, *Auctioning Animal Flesh: UK livestock markets*, Tonbridge, 1994

—, *Silencing the Lambs: UK lamb and sheep industry*, Tonbridge, 1995

The Association for the Study of Animal Behaviour, *Stimulus Response*, Cambridge, 1995

British Union for the Abolition of Vivisection (BUAV), *Health with Humanity*, London, 1988

Compassion in World Farming (CIWF), *Agony of Pigs*, Petersfield, 1990

—, *Calves in the Dock*, Petersfield, 1991

—, *Hens Might Fly*, Petersfield, 1991

—, *The Road to Misery*, Petersfield, 1992

—, *For a Few Pennies More*, Petersfield, 1994

The Humane Society of the United States, *Silent World: Genetic engineering*

Klaper, M., *A Diet for All Reasons: The health of vegans*, USA, 1995

People for the Ethical Treatment of Animals (PETA), *Unnecessary Fuss*, Washington, DC, 1984

—, *Britches*, Washington, DC, 1986

—, *Inside Biosearch*, Washington, DC, 1988

The Vegan Society, *Truth or Dairy*, St Leonards on Sea, 1994

Viva! (Vegetarians International Voice for Animals), *Viva! The Vegan/Vegetarian Issues*, Crewe, 1996

◆ INDEX